Judy

KAKEMBO:

A Heart Connection

God is good!!

Verna

KAKEMBO:

A Heart Connection

VERNA R DENO

XULON ELITE

Xulon Press Elite
2301 Lucien Way #415
Maitland, FL 32751
407.339.4217
www.xulonpress.com

Paperback ISBN-13: 978-1-66287-487-1
Ebook ISBN-13: 978-1-66287-488-8

FOREWORD

VERNA DENO BEGINS her story with a suspicious online meeting of a young African man. It developes into a complex, deeply caring relationship with him, thirty-three orphans, and the care-givers he calls family.

Verna journals this adventure, recounting her doubts, fears, prayers, and joys. Over time, a very tender, devoted, and trusting relation-ship is firmly established. Verna is eventually able to enjoy a flesh-and-blood meeting with these beautiful orphans and young adults in an exuberantly joyful Ugandan welcome!

There are many twists and turns in this journey. It travels through misgivings, angsts, successes, failures, prayers, and decisions with life-and-death outcomes.

God's providence shows up in many surprising ways!

Through Verna, God has also reached out to others and connected them with these compassionate, fun-loving young adults and their delightful children. The connection keeps expanding as hearts touch other hearts.

Verna's journey continues as life unfolds in this amazing, tightly-knit family of orphans. New developments, opportunities, needs, and threats are nonstop. There seems to never be enough resources to meet even the basic necessities; it can be an emotional roller coaster to prioritize essentials.

God claims a special relationship to widows, orphans, and the hungry. He adds a special blessing to those who are willing to stand in the gap on His behalf.

As this journey progresses, I am amazed at the ongoing accomplishments that happen through this "heart connection." What little we give, by our culture's standard, is multiplied many times over in poverty-stricken central Africa. Lives have been saved, fears quelled, children fed and clothed, a children's home built, and future church planters and pastors are trained. This is truly a God assignment!

Bob Deno

Husband of Author

INTRODUCTION

I SMILED AS I gazed at the beautiful faces. I cherish these engaging photos of the precious children and their devoted caregivers!

Little did I know how close I had come to throwing away such a wonderful opportunity for adventure and blessings beyond my wildest dreams!

African Apprehensions

THE LOUD "DING" of my Messenger alert startled me in the silence of the evening. While noting it, I thought, "Who is this guy? Kakembo Ian? I'd never heard of such a name."

His name was shown as a "Facebook friend" of a trusted evangelist, so I responded, "Hello."

"Hello my dear, how are you?" Kakembo asked.

"My dear"? His greeting set off warning bells in my mind. Was he trying to coax my good side? His profile showed he was a director and treasurer of an orphanage in Mityana, Uganda. That raised my eyebrow. I had never heard of the place and had read online about orphanage scams.

I responded, "Fine. How are you?"

"I greet you, sister, in the mighty name of Jesus," was his reply. "How is your day today?"

"Fine," was my curt reply. I wondered right away if his sweet words might be a hook to rope me into giving to a fraudulent scheme. So much for the small talk. I got right to business and began typing a series of questions based on his profile. "How are you acquainted

1

with my friend?" "...What church are you connected to?" "...How was your orphanage founded?" He answered the questions typing as fast as he could.

I continued. "How did you become director? "...How many children are there?" "...Where in the world is Mityana?" He again replied as thoroughly as he could while typing his responses, at times, in broken English.

It seemed the orphanage was independently founded by his pastor, Pastor Ssemwogelere, who was now in his seventies. The pastor had given the duties of heading the orphanage to him and his younger brother, Joseph. Kakembo claimed they had over thirty orphans they cared for.

Although Kakembo was his surname, or clan name, in Uganda, he said that was the name he went by. It is not uncommon in Uganda to be called by one's clan name. However, his brother used Ian as his first name.

Pastor Ssemwogelere had picked up Kakembo and Joseph off the streets. They had no father, and their mother was dying. The pastor and his wife took the boys into his home to be cared for. Kakembo was seven, and Joseph was four.

As the boys grew older, they began bringing more orphans to the pastor's small church with them.

I still had lots of unknowns in my mind on that August summer day of 2021, and a feeling of apprehension came to me when the conversation turned to the needs of the orphanage. Kakembo shared how the COVID-19 crisis had shut down churches and businesses in the area for many months, going on for two years. As a result, needs were very great with little food, no clean water, and lots of illness and disease. Malaria and typhoid was common, I was told.

I wondered if all he said was true. I had little knowledge about Uganda as a country.

I decided to read up on Mityana. It was a town with about 50,000 people in central Uganda with many outlying villages surrounded by agriculture.

It received a substantial amount of rain but had moderately warm temperatures year round. Photos showed it looking quite poor with very shabby buildings. Several articles commented about the thousands of orphans in the area and confirmed what Kakembo had stated about the COVID-19 pandemic having left many orphanages badly hurting for support.

I checked with my evangelist friend to see if he had ever met Kakembo. He hadn't. Could he verify the orphanage? He couldn't.

I read more information online warning people about orphanage scams in Africa. There were reports of children who were beaten, neglected, and even used for sexual exploitation, all for the love of money. Some articles claimed that the licensed orphanages were, at times, exploited by government officials for bribes. Others used the children to raise donations but neglected their basic needs.

I had doubts, but the orphanage stayed on my mind. During a very restless night, I asked, "Ok Lord, is this orphanage for real, or should I ignore him? Is this Kakembo guy trustworthy?"

I wanted to delete and forget the text conversation. Nevertheless, thinking that maybe . . . perhaps . . . this was a "God thing," I continued to read his messages.

Kakembo stated that he was a born-again Christian and a director of Mother of Hope Orphanage in Mityana, Uganda. Mother of Hope? Evangelical? I noted there was a Mother of Hope Hospital in the town as I looked at a rough map of the area.

The internet had very little information about the town, but my online reading confirmed that COVID-19 had indeed shut down area churches and charities for almost two years. My reading revealed the dire situation in Uganda, and orphanages were hit hard.

It didn't take long before Kakembo began to share with me his deep concern for one of his boys who was fighting malaria. "He may die due to lack of funds! The hospital will not treat him now since we have no more money," he pleaded.

"So . . . then . . . how could you afford a cell phone?" I asked suspiciously. The Facebook page revealed he had a cell number, and he was using it for Facebook and Messenger. "It is old. I received this phone four years ago for my birthday," he replied.

I checked a website that verified that Ugandan hospitals do not service patients unless funds for medical procedures are up-fronted **before** hospital care is given. The article pointed out that the poor in Uganda often could not provide medical care for their loved ones. If they did not have assets to sell, they were forced to watch a family member die! Even easily treated illnesses brought death simply due to the lack of money for medicines.

I earnestly began to check out things further. Searches resulted in sketchy information, but I pursued it. Yet doubts persisted. Kakembo was also listed as the treasurer of the orphanage on his Facebook page. I spoke frankly in the next message: "You realize that in the Bible, Judas was a treasurer!"

"No, no, dear sister! Please! I am not like that!" he responded. "I am a good man! I will do anything for these children! Anything!"

I continued reading about the many orphanage schemes in that country. My family members firmly reinforced my doubtful thinking.

In the nighttime, however, I wasn't so convinced. Scammer, Lord? Maybe not. His eyes? The photos he sent showed him with attractive and sincere brown eyes and a contagious beautiful smile!

And the children . . . so many beautiful children! They were, without a doubt, in need. His photos revealed their bare feet and poor clothing. But were they genuinely his photos?

Kakembo continued to reach out to me, generally at night due to the ten-hour time difference.

"Just ignore him!" said my husband, Bob, as I complained about my lack of sleep the next morning.

"Ok, alright. I'll do that!" I thought to myself. "Yes, I'll do that! Whew!" Suddenly I felt like I could let go of this! "I am, in truth, only obeying my husband," I reflected convincing myself.

I let it go for the remainder of the day, but moments after my head hit the pillow, nightly thoughts swirled in my mind nonstop. "What if he is genuine? He looks genuine. The children look so sweet! Oh stop this, Verna! Let it go! I can't be bothered by this! I'm tired, and I need my sleep!" I mumbled to myself. I turned up my sound machine to the ocean waves as I swallowed a couple more sleep aid tablets.

Sleep didn't come easily the next few nights. Slowly but surely, I began to listen to Kakembo's pleas. "Did you receive the pictures I sent you about our boy needing treatment?" he asked. I had received the photo of Kasumba, an orphanage boy.

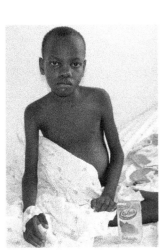
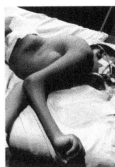

I was told he was in the hospital dying of malaria. He had also sent photos of the dated Mityana Hospital statements diagnosing malaria and the prescribed treatments with the required amount needed. Perhaps he really was out of money to pay to continue it?

"It seems authentic," I mumbled to myself. I had hoped it would have been an obvious scam so that I could drop the whole thing.

The next morning's message pleaded, "Please, Mom Verna. I have been praying so hard to talk to you again. You're the only one listening to me! Please, please don't let the boy die . . . Most people don't want to hear or see us . . . we are only poor people."

I noted his referencing me as "Mom" and thought of 1 Timothy 5:2, "Treat . . . older women as mothers . . ." I assumed it was the way of addressing older women in his church. Or maybe it wasn't? "Let the boy die"? Maybe this was his strategy to play on my emotions, or maybe not? Is this You, Lord, laying this burden on me? Or is it Kakembo? Or is it me?" My thoughts were nonstop. I couldn't shut out Kakembo's pleas.

I would only learn later that Kakembo and his brother, Joseph, had earlier held one of their dear orphans as he died in their arms. They were helpless to save him. They could not afford the medicines. As many of the poor in Uganda, they, too, knew all too well how easily death comes simply for lack of money. I had read that Malaria was one of the leading causes of death for children in Africa.

To find emotional relief, get some sleep at night, and stop these conversations once and for all, I agreed to send the modest funds. Kakembo instructed me on ways to do so. The payment to the hospital would need to be converted from dollars to shillings, and funds were transferred. It wasn't long after I received his thanks, saying, "Am so really happy . . . am going to pay Kasumba's balance so that he can receive his medicines."

His following photos showed the correctly dated Mityana Hospital bill. "Paid in Full" was displayed, showing the shillings amount equal to the money I had sent him. It was legitimate.

Messages of deep gratitude came flowing in from Kakembo. "Thank you so much for this miracle! Thank you . . . thank you so much for saving Kasumba's life . . . Truly this is a miracle!"

"Wow! 'Miracle'? " I thought to myself. "One rather small financial transaction that had no detrimental effect on our comfort level, not in the least, and it was received as a miracle on his end!" The thought humbled me. At the same time, I was so relieved my good deed was done. This would finally end our conversations!

KIDNEY QUANDARIES

"**MOM VERNA, I** am in the hospital feeling too bad in my stomach. I am in great pain, and the doctor has told me I am having kidney failure," Kakembo's message read several weeks later. "What! Kidney failure! No way! This has got to be a scheme!" As I shared details with my husband, he assured me it must be a scam.

"Just delete the messages and forget this Kakembo guy!" he answered me abruptly.

That was enough, and frankly, it didn't take much at that point to convince me. I just could not believe that now Kakembo himself had a life-threatening disease! And so soon after the last malaria episode!

Nevertheless, during the night when his messages came, and for some unknown reason, even to me, I felt obliged to explain to him why I was now choosing to block him. "I have read about all the scams your way, and I have good reason to believe you are a scammer!" I reported. "I want to stop all contact with you!"

"No, Mom Verna! No! I am a good man of God! I am a good man! I can prove it to you with videos! I can send you videos and photos! Please, I cannot do this without your support and prayers! I desperately, desperately need your help! Please don't leave us!"

Wow, I wished he didn't sound so sincerely in despair! "Lord," I prayed, "I really need verification of Your will in all of this!"

"Mom Verna, the clinic has diagnosed me with kidney failure! I will die without help! I truly need your help!" The photo of his ultrasound diagnosis confirmed it.

It was too much for me to deal with at the time. We were in the middle of helping our daughter and son-in-law relocate and move out. They would be living with us, and we would help them as they searched for a house and began new jobs.

I responded, "I am sorry, but I am unable to help at this time." I knew in my heart that was not true. Nevertheless, I asked him to please find help elsewhere. I had too much on my plate.

A verse came into my mind, "Do not withhold good from those to whom it is due, when it is in your power to act. Do not say to your neighbor, 'Come back tomorrow and I'll give it to you' when you already have it with you." (Proverbs 3:27-28). I pushed it out of my mind.

In his gentle Ugandan manner, Kakembo replied, "Ok, Mom. I will try and find help, and I don't want to put you on my burden. It's not compulsory that you have to suffer because of me if it's too much for you to help.

" . . . please don't worry. I know the Lord has a reason why all this is happening, and if he wishes to take my life, its ok . . . it will be His decision.

"I don't want you to be bothered cause I know you have much to handle. Am just a poor man, and I know we people have not much to say . . . He decides, but we will do our best . . . Thank you for taking the time to talk to me."

I was taken aback by his sincere humility! Why does he have to sound so genuine?" I grumbled. It reminded me of Proverbs 21:13, "Whoever shuts their ears to the cry of the poor will also cry out and not be answered." Ouch!

"Great! So much for getting a sound sleep tonight!" I grumbled to myself.

I continued to feel misgivings about my decision not to help. Bob eventually read Kakembo's text conversations. The desperation of this young man's messages finally got Bob to rethink the situation. The photos of the X-rays and doctor's reports that ensued cemented the validity of it all in Bob's mind, and he finally gave me the go-ahead to help.

He advised me that I contact the Mityana Hospital directly for verification, so I sent an email, and they answered back, confirming that Ian Kakembo had indeed been admitted as a patient with an extremely urgent need for kidney removal. Money would need to be collected **before** the surgery could begin. Oh, no! I had forgotten that total payment had to come first! It was a significant sum of money. Nevertheless, it was far less than a kidney surgery in the US.

FINANCIAL FIASCOS

REQUIRING THE SIGNIFICANT amount upfront for urgent surgery seemed like extortion, unlike our American hospitals! I felt irate! I sent an email to the hospital business office expressing my disdain for their ways and let them know, in no uncertain terms, my displeasure, and I suggested they take monthly payments!

I quickly learned that my righteous indignation bore absolutely no weight to them! Zilch! I winced at their response, totally ignoring the passion with which I sent my email. They succinctly expressed that the **total** amount of money had to be prepaid **before** medication and surgery. In addition, funds had to come as soon as possible due to its urgency. ASAP! My prestigious American influence and persuasiveness had as much impact as a fly hitting the windshield of a Mac truck!

In the interim, I tried contacting charities with international influence. Could they help in this urgent situation for the director of this orphanage? I was flying off emails right and left. Several answered back. Most didn't reply. Any responses were simply an apology explaining that they were inundated with overwhelming world needs for assistance at this time, and they could not help. No doubt, there were indeed so many world needs in this day and age.

I checked with other orphanages and charities in the area of Mityana, Uganda. Still no response. I inquired with Christian charitable organizations in the US, but the response always seemed the same. They were already so overwhelmed with needs, and they couldn't consider it at that time. Really? It was beginning to look like the Lord was placing this squarely on Bob and my shoulders.

I then rashly decided to send the entire amount needed for the surgery. The Xoom app looked simple enough. However, after wiring the transaction, I apparently and inadvertently sent off a series of fraud alerts! A significant sum of money sent to poor Uganda was suspect enough for a fraud, I was told, not to mention being suspect of funding terrorism! I learned later that I had also indicated my country as being the UK instead of the US. That sure didn't alleviate things!

In addition to that, my credit card company decided it was in my best interest to lock up my account! Unbelievable! I had already communicated to Kakembo that the funds were coming to him by that next morning. As he lay helpless on his hospital bed, my news of the subsequent halted funds dashed Kakembo's hopes and spirit!

I tried a different means, Western Union. I immediately received the message that the transaction went through. "Whew!" I thought. However, within hours, I received another alert that the funds had been stopped! Again? Obviously, Western Union and Xoom talked to each other! Fraud was suspected due to the previous fraud alert.

"Mom, am really afraid . . . I have severe pain. I am afraid I am going to die!" messaged Kakembo in my night hours. Joseph, Kakembo's brother, was now at his side in the hospital. Within days, Kakembo had become so weak he was unable to talk or text. He was also in excruciating pain.

I spoke with Joseph via Messenger chats. For each of my two initial rushed messages promising the life-giving funds, he was required to walk over two miles to get to the bank. He would briskly walk the long trek to only arrive and receive the foreboding message that funds had been undeliverable! My two failed attempts were like a punch in the gut for Joseph! Each unsuccessful transaction left him totally disillusioned while meandering back to the hospital to be by his older brother's side.

"I have got to buy you two a bicycle!" I cried to Joseph. I was witnessing a huge amount of wasted time and energy for him just to reach the bank, and on an empty stomach at that! Joseph had vowed to God that he would fast and eat nothing until Kakembo received his surgery.

Needless to say, I was feeling the pressure. In my third method, via WorldRemit, I was sent a message that the money had indeed deposited into their bank account to pay for the surgery. Finally! It seemed the urgent funds went through, and quickly!

"Praise God Almighty for this miracle! We thank you more than words can say!" replied Joseph as I assured him the funds were transmitted successfully.

But, no! Ughhh! Yet again! The payment had been stopped! His two-mile walk to the bank did absolutely nothing but exhaust him and only proved that my promises would go totally unfulfilled! Not a cent of the surgery funds had been delivered! I was now the one to look like the fraudster, the deceiver, the scammer! So far, hollow and empty promises were all I had provided!

"**Why** God?" I called out. I had attempted three consecutive days to send this money, and each time after receiving notice that the funds had sent, I was subsequently notified that the transaction had failed. I had learned that Kakembo was undergoing extreme suffering and was receiving absolutely **no** pain medications due to cost!

Joseph cried out to me in the night, "We promised the hospital and the surgeon that the funds would come, and there is none! Three times I have gone to the bank, and each time the money was not there! The doctor had made an incision to release fluid pressure, but they are not giving medicines since they have not received payment . . . We have no money for the pain! They are beginning to believe we are liars!" Joseph went on.

"His wounds are becoming infected! He is in great pain! The wound is decaying and giving out a bad smell! They will not give clean bandages without first getting the money . . . I can't live without my brother! He means so very much to me! The children are crying and missing him so much! He is our everything at the orphanage and to the community!"

I am fasting and praying until Kakembo gets treated . . . Oh God, why is this happening?" Joseph pleaded.

"Indeed, Lord! Why is this happening?" I prayed out loud.

Joseph's cries became markedly desperate. "There is no reason to live without my brother! This is too painful to watch!" His messages continued into the wee hours of the morning.

Joseph, watching his dearly beloved brother groaning in agonizing pain, could take no more. Kakembo was slowly dying right before his eyes. I did my best to encourage him to hang on. "I'm not a miracle worker, but God will not fail!" I gave Scripture verses to try and sustain him in the night. "Don't give up, Joseph!" I implored, adding, "I am not giving up, so please, don't you give up on me!" Yet, beneath my courageous cheerleading front, I, too, felt extremely helpless.

Kakembo had previously shared that Pastor Ssemwogelere and his wife had started a small independent evangelical church years ago, as well as the orphanage. Though poorly built, a generous man in Mityana had donated the orphanage building.

He turned over the pastoral and orphanage duties to Kakembo and Joseph due to the stress of the Covid-19 pandemic. The pastor currently has a small farm that he and his wife try to manage. It was his intention to entirely hand over the orphanage and building to Kakembo and Joseph when the Lord chose to take him home.

Due to his age and the pandemic, the pastor's ministry had been stopped short. His age left little strength, and his health wasn't good. Pastor Ssemwogelere still does evangelistic outreaches, however, in outlying villages as his health allows.

Food and orphanage supplies waned with the pandemic. Kakembo, with Joseph's help, was given directorship of the orphanage, along with pastoral duties. These two young men were now on their own.

The church and nearby community members who had, in pre-COVID-19 times, given food and assistance to the orphanage, were not able to help. Kakembo found himself unable to offer food assistance to the older community of women and widows who had once depended on him. He had talked about the unfed orphans in the streets, and it broke his heart knowing he was helpless to provide for their needs. Indeed, my reading about Mityana verified that there were many street orphans in the town and surrounding areas during COVID-19.

The COVID-19 shutdown policies devastated businesses as well as orphanages. Kakembo was given a real taste of how very deep and heavy this burden was and what a huge responsibility it would be to feed and care for thirty-three orphans and three adults.

Food was very scarce! Corn flour mush became their only food source when available. Water was a long two-mile walk to a murky and swampy stream where The children would help carry jerry cans for bathing and cooking. Drinking water needed to be purchased, and there was little money. The bathroom situation of latrines with no running water also aided the spread of illness and disease.

The children were gloomy, and any hope for their dear Kakembo returning to the orphanage was waning daily due to his kidney failure. Countless tears were flowing as they missed him at the orphanage.

I got very little sleep at night as I struggled during the daylight hours trying to resolve the funding problems. My husband, Bob, began to see the utter desperation of Kakembo as I continued to share the messages and photos with him.

Validated Determination

IT HAS BEEN my experience in my fifty years of walking with the Lord that in my most desperate stages of life, God would reach into my inner being as I cried out to Him. As I look back, He has never failed me.

It was in frantic times that I came to know Him anew as my Savior as He pulled me out of my own strength and replaced it with His. As hard as it was in those times, it would always amaze me how wonderful His grace was when He came through for me. Kakembo and Joseph would experience the Lord's grace as well in their most desperate moments.

That Sunday while preaching, our pastor shared photos of his prior mission to Haiti. It was difficult watching the scenes of poverty and misery among the jam-packed shanties in what seemed like a sea of humanity. His message was on the rich man and Lazarus. The rich man, showing no love or compassion, was completely indifferent to the plight of the extremely poor Lazarus. Eventually, both died. Lazarus went to the glories of paradise. The rich man went to the torments of hades.

How easy it is for Americans to turn away and tune out to the needs and pleas of the poor. While we comfortably take in our comfort and leisure, we convince ourselves it's too big of a problem to help.

There are vast populations in the world who are desperately hungry! Many, as I was, are persuaded that it's much like throwing a teaspoon of water into an enormously dry desert, so why try?

Bob and I somberly left church that morning. Yet we were gratified that we had made a definite decision to help Kakembo. The message validated our determination to go ahead and help in this dire situation. We were doing the right thing, and we were glad, maybe even a bit relieved, that we were able to leave feeling confirmed in our efforts rather than convicted!

Our fourth attempt at sending funds was eventually done directly by our bank and with success! However, a daily maximum amount and possible three-day delay for each payment to arrive made a postponement that complicated matters. Kakembo needed help at that present moment, not three days later! I wanted to avoid this but felt that everything was going in slow motion! My patience and endurance were threadbare. Would the direly-needed dollars get there in time? Would Kakembo make it and live to see another day?

The situation was becoming intolerable. Joseph had begged for the hospital to give pain medication to Kakembo. However, his previous promises of payments that were never delivered made the hospital even more adamant. They reiterated, no money, no medicine!

With no guarantee of timely arrival, the funds were finally sent by bank-to-bank transfer. My praying greatly intensified. My anxiety was high and, unfortunately, my hopes were low. "God has never failed me. God has never failed me. He is my help in time of trouble," I kept reminding myself.

Contagious Joy!

THE NEXT DAY, I heard the familiar "ding" alert of Facebook Messenger. I was so dreading to hear from Joseph. I wasn't sure I could handle more bad news, so I braced myself.

"Thank you, thank you, thank so much! I'm so happy! I'm so happy!"

I was astounded by Joseph's words!

"I'm praising God, and I danced all the way back to the hospital after collecting the money! I have done somersaults in the air . . . I'm so happy! We got you from heaven . . . from God, and we are so, so thankful for you! Thank you, God, for your mercy to us! Thank you, God," he continued.

It was months later that I actually viewed a video showing this young athletic man doing a series of backflips! He wasn't joking when he said he did somersaults in the air!

I laughed out loud at the intensity of Joseph's response! An incredible, almost magical surge of joy filled my heart. Finally, Kakembo could now receive pain medication and have his wound cleaned and bandaged! Surgery could be scheduled right away!

Medication would be administered! A literal divine infusion of hope began to rise in Joseph and Kakembo's hearts and mine too! I felt like dancing, and I did! What an ordeal we had gone through!

Kidney removal surgery was scheduled immediately, and the medication would be administered.

"Praise God, praise God. Thank you, Lord! You are so good! Your mercies are new every morning! We love You, Lord, so much!" Huge relief, joy, and gratefulness overwhelmed my heart.

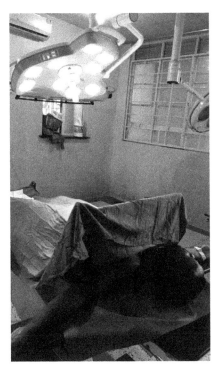

Surgery was precarious. There were complications due to the delay. Joseph was actually able to video part of the surgery in action. As

we viewed it, we noticed the degree of disintegration along the floor and walls of the simple operating room. Bob was amazed by the fact that they even allowed Joseph to be there to film it! My husband was skeptical of the outcome of this surgery. But in the end, the surgeon proved he was very competent, and God proved His provision, mercy, and grace.

Kakembo would then begin the weeks-long process of recovery. It would take longer than normal due to the delay of surgery. After several days, I was surprised to hear the familiar ding of Messenger that morning. Kakembo was alert enough to do a video chat with Joseph's help! "I am so grateful to the Lord and to you for helping me! May the Lord bless you endlessly, and may the Lord give you everything in life and bless your family for this miracle! Thank you, thank you, so much, Mom Verna!" His voice was extremely weak, but it was so very wonderful to see his face and hear that faint voice!

We were able to have live video chats the following several weeks. "I am just so happy to have someone who cares about me and the children, Mom . . . The Lord has shown His mercy on us! I can't wait to go back and see the kids and their happy faces when they see me again! I will call you on that day so you can see the happiness on everyone's faces! Hahaha, I will shout hallelujah and laugh so loud and shout out what the Lord has done for me!"

Kakembo has a beautiful laugh, and he laughed loudly. A joy I hadn't experienced before filled my heart at the sound of his voice! His joy was so contagious!

As I began to experience the inmost heart and love of Jesus through Kakembo, it humbled me. This newly found relationship would connect me further to Christ's deep heart and divine love.

Kakembo's following message read, "The Lord is doing so much! He has given me another chance to take care of the kids and everybody who needs my help in the community. I will do the Lord's work again. But this time I will be doing it with ALL my heart because now I know I am here for a purpose! My dream is that one day I will meet you and give you a big hug!"

"Me too, dearest Kakembo, me too," I thought to myself.

In the meantime, during the healing process while Kakembo slept, Joseph and I were planning a welcome-back party for him. "The children love you a lot, and I can't wait to make a video call with you when Kakembo returns," Joseph continued excitedly. "All in the community are waiting to welcome him back!"

It would be a simple party. The funds I provided would only be enough for cake, drinks, and a chicken and rice meal. Meat had been scarce for them, so it was eagerly received!

In a week or so, Kakembo became well enough to walk in the hospital. He started to visit and pray with other patients. "Every day I have to walk in my ward to meet other patients in the hospital, and I tell them the gospel of Jesus Christ and pray for them as well. Many patients are becoming born again to Jesus, Mom, when I tell them all that the Lord has done for me! I give them my testimony how the Lord has given me a second chance to live! I can't stop teaching about how wonderful He is and how merciful He is! I'm not ashamed to shout hallelujah in a loud voice!"

God was indeed using this young servant of Christ, and his passion for the Lord was so contagious, especially to me. His testimony reminds me of Psalm 40:2–3, one I have prayed many times, "He lifted me out of the slimy pit, out of the mud and mire. He set my feet on a rock and gave me a firm place to stand. He put a new song in my mouth, a hymn of praise to our God. Many will see and fear the Lord and put their trust in Him." Kakembo was, in fact, a living testimony to that.

The day finally arrived for Kakembo's return to the orphanage. As I watched the live videos and photos sent to me, I beamed. I saw such happiness, and it made my heart glad.

Kakembo told me he had a little surprise for me. I laughed out loud when I saw it: a framed photo of me he had used from an older Facebook post. "Wow that's one **young** version of me!"

He walked and showed another photo of Bob and me hanging on the wall. "Here's one of you and Dad Bob," he continued. "We want the kids to know your faces. They love you so much for bringing me back to them alive!"

It was very humbling to hear his words, yet I felt truly honored. Kakembo's joyful exuberant love of God and the children was beginning to endear Kakembo more and more to my heart.

The happy children's voices and laughter was music to my ears! Joseph panned the camera, and I saw children swarming all around

Kakembo with glee and love. Undoubtedly, they had missed him so very much!

Little did I know how special these servants of Christ in Uganda would become to Bob and me.

Kakembo seeks direction from me when disciplining the kids, in financial matters, spiritual matters, and even matters of the heart. The photos and videos he sends of the children reaffirm in our hearts the reasons we give. We are indeed learning the veracity of Acts

20:35b, "We must help the weak, remembering the words the Lord Jesus himself said: 'It is more blessed to give than to receive.'"

Bob and I often remark at how much joy we have in our lives through this heart connection: the lives of these precious orphans and two young men who were once orphans themselves.

MINI MIRACLES

OUR MESSENGER TEXTS continued. I noted that temperatures were getting cooler at night in Mityana, according to my web search. I asked Kakembo, and he shared with me that the weather dropped to about sixty-four degrees at night, and the children were sharing blankets.

Schools were still in closure mode due to the pandemic. Bob and I thought it wise to provide funds for blankets and books for the children. Kakembo responded with his familiar words, "It's a miracle! Thank you so much!" Photos of him and the children wrapped in the blankets and receipts of the purchases followed.

I was taken by surprise when Kakembo shared his recent photos with his thankful acknowledgments. I assumed he would buy storybooks for the kids, but his photos and receipts indicated that he had bought textbooks.

I gave some thought as I looked at the photos. Again, a rather insignificant gift on our part was, in fact, a true miracle on Kakembo's end! No major inconveniences came to us with this gift; it was an inconsequential amount and required little effort from us. Yet it was so very important to Kakembo and the orphanage. Warmth and education were not taken for granted by him.

I, however, had taken these gifts without any appreciation throughout my entire life! I really don't think I have **ever** thanked God for a textbook, let alone a blanket! I began to think about how very, very little I had acknowledged the Lord for His miracles in my own life.

Kakembo's gratitude affected me, as even a small gift on this side of the world can be so important to these precious children on their side of the world. What wonder I have deferred by ignoring and not allowing awe and wonder for His surprises and provisions in my own life's journeys!

I learned that later Kakembo even found a teacher who was willing to come to the orphanage to teach. He was set on the children getting educated while the schools were closed due to COVID-19, and they had been closed for some time. Clearly, the children's best interests were at the forefront of Kakembo's mind.

I cherished the ongoing photos and videos that were regularly sent of the kids working and playing. Their appreciation of our gifts were demonstrated in videos by their chorus of, "Thank you, thank you, thank you! We love you so much!" Needless to say, their bright smiles brought big smiles to our faces as well! Bob and I also appreciated his pictures of each dated purchase receipt verifying that our every gift was spent for the purpose we had sent it. He was meticulous in providing proof to us.

Our trust in Kakembo grew as time went on. He proved to be a dedicated, hardworking "true blue" servant of Christ with an obvious love and concern for his children.

"I am so happy that you made it possible for me to provide blankets and books for the kids!" Kakembo wrote, adding "I will rest now because it has been a long day walking and shopping . . . like seven miles."

"Seven miles!" I responded. "I'd be doing good to walk three miles!" It was evident that his hard work and sacrifice for the well-being of the children was who he was. I couldn't help but be attracted to his devotion. The heart of the Lord was clearly visible in this young and strong servant.

I remember asking the Lord, "Wow Lord, where are You taking me with all this!" It seemed that I heard a whispered reply, "Don't worry, Verna. Just follow your heart."

Backstory

A **little about** my background: I remember early in our marriage when Bob and I had followed our hearts in another direction. We have had quite a variety of adventures throughout our fifty years of marriage.

In our early years in Spokane, Washington, we were easily blessed with good jobs. Bob had no problem getting on the Spokane Fire Department after his stint in Vietnam with the Marine Corps. I worked as a legal secretary right out of high school. All those classes in typing and shorthand paid off for me!

We were both just beginning to grow in our newfound faith in Christ, but it came with a lot of marital bumps and bruises along the way!

During the first three years of marriage, the Lord opened our eyes to the world of missions through our church. We were awe-inspired with missionary visitors in church, some with incredible stories of faith.

One particular Sunday during a missions conference, we listened to an amazing testimony of a woman missionary and her fascinating stories of her ministry in Africa. The service ended with an altar call to invite anyone with a yearning to serve the Lord in missions to come forward. The Lord was pulling at both of our hearts. Bob and

I looked at each other, and with a little nudging on my part, we took each other's hand and walked the aisle to the front. There we made a public confession that we wanted to serve the Lord in missions. What ensued now makes me dizzy to just think about it.

We seemingly threw caution to the wind and jumped into our new life purpose with both feet. We were adventurers at heart, but little did we know the cost. We eventually gave it our all by quitting our good jobs and selling our new home and furniture. After some Bible school training under our belts, Bob was counseled to consider going to seminary.

We both came from blue-collar working families. It left our parents in unbelief! I can only imagine how they must have felt. I'm sure that in their minds, they were thinking we were throwing our great future away. Both of our parents, however, would never stand in our way and eventually resigned to the fact that we weren't going to change our minds. There were loads of tears as we said our final goodbyes.

Bob's three years of intensive biblical training at Denver Seminary while working part-time jobs and my full-time work left us emotionally and physically spent, and the time it took for the two of us to actually lay a good spiritual marriage foundation was in short supply.

Bible knowledge may have been going into the mind, but it was quite another thing to live it out! Spiritual development was a rough go. Neither one of us grew up in homes where Christ and faith were central to life.

Learning to rely on the Lord's Word and His grace was learned in baby steps with a lot of falls and getting back up again! When we were finally received as candidates three years later to be missionaries in Italy, our baby steps morphed into giant steps! It wouldn't be long before we would take the full plunge into living by faith as we would raise support and begin to depend entirely on God's grace through the charity of the Lord's people.

That was a very difficult time for me. Transferring ourselves from independent, self-sufficient wage-earners to becoming dependent recipients of the good hearts of Christian people took some emotional mind-bending! It never came naturally for me. I wanted the safety net of a secure monthly salary. Living by faith was a whole different ballgame!

There were many other safety nets that were pulled out from under me as well. We were venturing into a different culture, a new world, where my very identity as an American would fade into the world of a new language, new customs, new foods, and a completely new environment.

The Lord had to teach me many things, especially about humility. I would, in time, however, learn that the Lord faithfully provided for our every need, many times in totally unexpected ways!

In addition to these new learning curves, we were notified that our long wait to adopt a baby had miraculously arrived! We received Monica into our lives when she was just six weeks old.

We had been praying and waiting for five years of our ten-year marriage for a child. Life became more beautiful but also much more complicated for us as new parents. There was no nine-month preliminary induction. We were immersed into parenthood with little preparation! Along with that came an extended time of raising financial support as we traveled to many churches in different states. It was difficult and challenging to be a brand new mother while traveling to different towns and churches and staying in different homes during these eighteen months to raise our necessary funds. However, the day finally arrived! We would move to Italy for ministry.

ITALIAN MEMOIRS

WE BEGAN WITH a year of language learning and living in Florence, Italy, to prepare us for a church-planting ministry in Naples. We initially had to resort to Italian preschool for Monica while we did language training.

Little did we know at the time that Monica would spend a significant amount of her mornings sitting in a corner with her face to the wall. Years ago, this shaming technique was the Italian method used to control children, such as our defiant and frustrated toddler. However, it brought no remorse nor contrition into our little darling's heart. She picked up the irate phrases given to her and repeated them right back, offending many in the process!

After moving to Naples, I was amazed at the differences! Sophisticated and well-to-do Florentines had little to do with their boisterous, emotional, and flamboyant Neapolitan neighbors. Even the language was different. Florence, with its Renaissance masterpieces of art, is a classy and orderly city. Naples, on the other hand, was densely populated, noisy, and extremely chaotic.

Monica mistook these outgoing Neapolitan personalities with characteristically loud voices as if they were shouting at her. The nursery school days were, no doubt, a trigger, and the only time Bob and I used loud voices was at home when we were angry. So while misunderstanding their gregarious and loud greetings, she would vengefully wipe off every affectionate pinch given to her chubby cheeks! She refused their affectionate kisses altogether.

I learned firsthand what claustrophobia was as I shopped the extremely crowded Neapolitan open markets. Monica would cling to my leg, eating the dust as we paraded through the colorful displays of goods.

It was dusty and noisy! Theatrical vendors proudly used their vocal cords to advertise their goods, competing with their neighboring vendors. Some would spontaneously barrel out a passionate Italian love song while a vendor farther down would powerfully serenade and compete with a more recent ballad.

Parks were not to be found. Small cars and mopeds would weave in and out of the narrow cobblestone streets, many even using the sidewalks themselves to get around others. During our walks, brightly colored laundry would wave like flags above me as the apartment dwellers utilized their balconies with clotheslines. Women would compete with street noises by shouting from their balconies to a neighbor sharing the recent family news or juicy gossip.

Monica much preferred to travel via her dad. Bob walked many miles with Monica attached to his back. She thoroughly enjoyed swaying back and forth in the backpack while he forged his way through the busy and crowded streets.

The Camorra, an Italian Mafia-type criminal organization, ruled in Naples. A young Italian man, Paolo, who we knew well, had worked inside the Camorra. He would visit many shop owners who had to pay him "il pizzo," the protection money just to ensure their shop would not get hit by Camorra gangsters. He had come to know the Lord as his Savior during that time, and his life had been radically turned around! If there was one Neapolitan our daughter Monica loved, it was this dear young man! She adored Paolo!

We, however, came to a conclusion after our four-year term that the Neapolitan culture didn't mix well with our then four-year-old daughter. Nevertheless, the years were richly intertwined with many wonderful and deeply meaningful experiences as we lived with these life-grabbing, loving, heartfelt Neapolitans. The Lord was so good and allowed us to witness to many hearts who turned to Christ during our time there.

The Lord continues to supply us with His faith and love in uncertain times. Our cross-cultural missions experience has laid the foundation to embrace our new cultural adventures. Uganda is yet another country of vivacious and life-loving individuals! And oh how much I am learning to love these orphan care-givers and the thirty-three children under their care! We have new God-adventures awaiting us.

ALASKA ADVENTURES

NEW ADVENTURES AWAITED as we followed our hearts back to America. After Bob's five-year apprenticeship training to become a journeyman sheet metal mechanic, life was again secure with a good-paying trade. In later years, however, the recession hit the US in full force, and unemployment benefits became more of the norm, leaving us with very little money in the bank.

Months of lay-off lingered on until Alaska offered a short-term sheet metal job. We had little choice but for Bob to grab it. It was a 2300-mile driving trip for him to arrive to his new work site!

While Bob worked in far-away Alaska, I worked in Wenatchee, Washington, as a school office administrator. However, after over one long year of separation, we finally realized that this would not be a short-term job! I decided it was high time I joined my husband.

Once again, following our hearts, we decided to make the long distance a permanent move. It was extremely difficult, however, leaving our one and only newly-married twenty-three-year-old daughter over 2300 miles away! There was a flood of emotions and tears.

After only one and a half years of Alaskan residency, however, we were taken aback that job security and lay-offs, once again, began to impact our lives. After a very dry financial year and lots of prayer, the

Lord faithfully came through, as He always has for us. This time it was with a very secure and good job as foreman in the maintenance shop with the Anchorage School District. It seemed in our darkest moments, God opened the door and saved the best employment for last. It provided later for a good and secure retirement, which we had earlier lost all hope of ever attaining.

The Lord has always provided. In the earlier years of marriage when we had become hopeless about ever having a child of our own, He provided. Our beautiful daughter, Monica, was an extraordinary blessing through adoption!

Much later, the Lord added Ben, our wonderful son-in-law, to the package! The Lord has never failed to provide in any way, even through rough financial times. We know we can trust Him to supply for our needs as we meet the orphanage needs, and we look forward to His new adventures for us.

Mountain Mama

KAKEMBO HAD REVEALED to me that his spiritual life had been renewed and completely changed since his close call with death. His irreverent rap music-loving younger days had turned now to a more mature young man who longed for a closer and more personal walk with the Lord, and his conversations proved that to me.

After the familiar "ding" on my iPhone at about 6:00 p.m. Ugandan time, I was transported via video chat to a mountain side where Kakembo sat overlooking a vast landscape of bushes and low trees. The connection was poor. Nevertheless, we were able to message. "Did you walk to the mountain, or did someone give you a ride?" I asked.

"No, I walked, and to reach here is about six miles," he replied.

"Six miles!" I responded. "And you still have to walk back! That's incredible!" I exclaimed.

"Am used to walking long distance, Mom; am a strong man," was his reply. "I need to talk to the Lord on the mountain, Mom. God is good cause He has made everything possible. Am so grateful! Oh, all the glory to the Lord! I hope you like the mountain view, Mom."

"I love the mountain view!" I answered. Indeed mountains were my favorite place to be! I was born and grew up as a child with the Rocky Mountains surrounding my hometown of Eureka, Montana. Mountains were in my blood!

It was in our mid-thirties that Bob and I had become missionaries in Naples, Italy. Those years of dense chaotic city life left me literally yearning, almost desperately, for mountain walks! I would have never believed that some years later, we would be living, for over thirteen years, in the vast mountainous region of Alaska!

My daily fix of those intensely-gorgeous huge mountains of the Chugach Alaska Range would deeply satisfy my innermost soul's longings! The incredible awe of His creation overwhelmed me at times, and the sites of high glacier-capped pinnacles became even more inherent to my deepest needs of well-being.

We now live our retired life in Idaho, with winter stays in Arizona. Mountains are still an important and frequent part of our lives as we travel in Idaho, Washington, and Montana.

I am mesmerized, at times, by my memory photos of the many beautiful mountain walks we have enjoyed in our fifty years of marriage!

As we winter in Arizona, I have been pleasantly surprised to see the beautiful purple Santa Rita mountains surrounding Green Valley and the Sonoran Desert.

They are uniquely beautiful in Arizona style. Indeed my love of mountains are a deeply-rooted integral part of my being.

"How was your walk?" Kakembo inquired that evening. "Oh, it was great except the part where I had to carry Bob up the hill," I quipped.

"Hahaha, you're funny, Mom! I hope it was Dad Bob carrying you up that hill!" His reply made me chuckle.

Kakembo knew I loved mountains as much as he loved his prayer mountain. So when he signed off with, "Goodbye, dear mountain Mama, from your mountain son," I laughed! Yes! I was a mountain mama, for sure!

I was moved by Kakembo's discipline to go out of his way to fast and make time for God. Fasting wasn't a typical or consistent part of my Christian walk. However, Kakembo's example was rubbing off on me.

I have since been learning how valuable this spiritual resource is. It's proven to help bring me humility and a drawing to the Lord's heart.

Some have learned that to personally experience the presence of God, it's important to involve fasting and prayer. It has been physically proven that after a three or four-day fast, your brain will shut down the physical appetites, cutting off the hunger mode. What isn't understood in the secular mode is that for the follower of Christ, this discipline will also open your soul and spirit to hear His voice through His Word in a much clearer manner than normal.

Our secular society has capitalized on the overstimulation of the mind through busyness and media in today's world. As I learned more about this spiritual resource, this mountain mama has found mountains to be my favorite place for this type of spiritual retreat.

A Father's Heart

"HELLO, MY MOM. How are you doing?" Kakembo messaged.

"Hello, and how are you?" I replied.

"So bad, my Mom, all here are crying. I went to pick the rest of the blankets up today, and I received a call from Brenda, a child that got an accident at the orphanage. The kid fell into the cooking porridge!"

The stove they cooked on was basically a fire pit with a pot over it.

"Oh no, was he hurt?"

"Yes, Mom. Let me send you the pictures."

I shuddered as I saw the photo. "Oh, that's terrible! Have you got medicine? Are you taking him to the hospital?"

"We haven't got any medicine yet cause all the money I paid to the store for the blankets. But it's ok, I can go and take blankets back and see if they refund some money to treat the boy. Am feeling so bad. I can't stop blaming myself for this. Am really crying, Mom. The kids can't sleep. He is crying, and he's in so much pain tonight, Mom!"

I felt so badly for him and responded, "Don't blame yourself, son. Please take the child right away to get checked out by a doctor! What is his name?"

"He is called Buyondo Moses. I will take him early in the morning to the hospital." His photo of Joseph and Baby Moses confirmed the critical need of medical care!

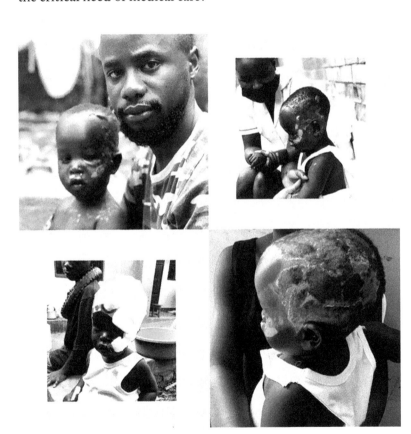

"Can you take him tonight? The earlier the better!" I was so worried for baby Moses! He was so young!

"I can do anything for him, Mom . . . anything . . . am so hurt . . . can't sleep . . . Let me take him right now, Mom, cause he's in so much pain! Let me rush him to the hospital with the help of Brenda and Joseph."

As a young adult, Brenda, is a very important and an essential help with the children. She was raised as an orphan since age four by Pastor and Mrs. Ssemwogelere.

This young woman does much of the cooking, cleaning, laundry, and teaching for the thirty-three kids. She loves the children deeply. She also has a zeal for evangelizing and sharing the good news of Jesus in their community. She is also very committed to helping Mrs. Ssemwogelere, the pastor's wife, during her times of health needs. She is a true daughter in Christ with a servant's heart.

Kakembo continued, "Brenda has fainted, Mom. She's crying too much! She has fainted two times, according to the kids. It's too much for her! Please pray for Brenda."

"Do you have a way to get to the hospital?" I asked.

"We don't have any means of transport at this late time of night. Joseph and I will just walk to the hospital." It was over several miles away in the dead of night!

"Oh my gosh," I thought to myself, "I have got to get them a bicycle!" My thoughts and communication continued in the following hours. It was ten hours later there than my time. After some hours, I messaged "Have you reached the hospital yet?"

"Mom, am here. We reached the hospital, and they are checking the baby. We had to stand in the veranda for hours to wait for a doctor."

"Oh you must be so tired," I responded.

"To be honest, I won't be able to sleep at all! The doctor told us the baby needs emergency treatment. I told him to do whatever is possible, to start giving him treatments, and I will pay him little by little. He has to save the baby from this pain, Mom!" I assured Kakembo not to worry about funds. Kakembo would be at the child's side for the entire night.

"They are starting to clean the wounds, Mom. Oh Lord, this is so painful! I can't watch this. I cannot bear to see my child facing so much pain, Mom! Oh, he is too young . . . oh Lord, help my boy! I can't stop crying for him, Mom. May the Lord have mercy on this innocent soul."

Kakembo needed my emotional support during the ordeal, and I stayed connected through my night hours. The very heart of Christ knitted our hearts together during baby Moses's suffering.

The Ugandan word for *son* is "mutabani." My "mutabani in Christ" was revealing his tender and fatherly heart toward this precious baby, demonstrating the deep love he had for the children under his care.

The next morning. I wanted to share the video of baby Moses to Bob. The child was crying badly as the nurses tried to clean the wounds. Bob refused to look! It was too painful even for him! It seemed that now there were three tender father types, Kakembo, Joseph, and Bob, caring so much for this sweet innocent child! Needless to say, we spent a good amount of time in prayer for baby Moses.

There was another Father who had to look away at the suffering of His innocent and pure Son. Jesus died on the cross for the sins of mankind crying, "Father, Father, why have you forsaken me!" It is said that this was part of the suffering that Jesus had to endure—to be absent from the Father and bear the sins of all of mankind on His shoulders alone. The heavenly Father looked away from His Son while He bore our sins to make a way for our eternal salvation. A holy God requires a holy sacrifice.

Sometimes I wonder, as the Father looked away, did he do it also because of the intense anguish of His heart? No doubt, He intensely felt the gut-wrenching and unimaginable suffering of His only pure and divine Son while Father God showed His wrath toward sin.

Surely, the almighty, heavenly Father has incredibly profound feelings, not only for His Son, but He also has intense feelings for each one of us as well! So much so, that He sent His only Son to suffer so we might have eternal life with Him.

His love is without limit! The great writer, A. W. Tozer, said, "Because God is self-existent, His love had no beginning. And because He is eternal, His love can have no end. Because He is infinite, it has no limit!" (Tozer, Knowledge of the Holy, 1961, p 98). Wow! No limit! Oh, how He loves you and me!

I reminded Kakembo that the mansion the Lord is preparing for him will be much grander than my mansion. My husband and I may have been giving seed to the sower, but he and the other dear adults were the ones doing the very hard work of sowing into the hard soil of Uganda!

The Bible teaches us to be poor in spirit. "Blessed are the poor in spirit for theirs is the kingdom of heaven." Matthew 5:3. I have much to learn about being poor in spirit. My US mid-class standard of well-being is in no way a measurement of my spirituality. The greatest of the Lord's gifts is love as 1Corinthians 13:13 reveals. "And now these three remain: faith, hope, and love. But the greatest of these is love."

I am witnessing and learning the profound depths of His love by the means of the very hearts of the "poor in Christ." Perhaps that is why it is often the poor, not the rich, who will go out of their way to give to another in need. The love of Christ runs deep in their empathetic hearts!

Bob and I experienced about three years of ministering to the poor in our early years of seminary in Denver, Colorado. We worked in an inner-city ministry among the poorest strata of the city.

We remember walking up the dilapidated steps of shabby apartments to visit families there. Mice ruled and didn't even bother moving out of our way as we ascended. As doors opened, we met poor pessimistic people who had very little hope for the future. However, through a series of interactions, showing respect, kindness, and love, we were able to draw some of them into the church. The transformation of the love of Jesus continued the process, and lives were changed! The challenge for us was representing this glorious love of the Lord in a way that they could see, feel, and experience.

Kakembo has committed himself to the devout care of the children. Brenda, Joseph, and he are the "poor in spirit" who depend on God's grace, mercy, and goodness for their daily provisions. Their love for these orphan children goes so deep! They are, in truth, family, bound together by the spiritual DNA of the blood of Jesus! It truly is a heart connection.

Spokes & Spigots

"**It has been** the best day ever, Mom!" Kakembo's message sounded so happy. "Baby Moses is coming home, and we are buying our bike!" Bob and I had made good on my promise, and we sent funds for a bicycle.

I thoroughly enjoyed the numerous photos and videos he sent. The big smiles on Kakembo, Joseph, and the children were so beautiful! His videos showed the bike loaded with two of the children hanging onto Kakembo for dear life, laughing gleefully as others trailed him, clinging to the back of the bike while running down the smooth clay path. I cracked up at the sight of such elated children who were totally oblivious to their precarious situation!

I realized that any other mom would have been a little horrified to see the risky scene with these little ones, but Kakembo looked totally in control, and he was! He would in no way allow any harm to his dear children.

"The kids are so happy for the bicycle . . . they are all out wanting rides on it . . . hahaha!" I was so delighted watching the scene! It gave me a deep satisfaction to watch the children having fun.

There were also functional uses for the bike. "It was so nice for us having a ride and using it to fetch water," Kakembo mentioned.

Meanwhile, he was sending photos of the kids filling yellow jerry cans at the very murky water springs. It was the only source of water for the poor in the area villages. I intently watched the video of the children balancing yellow-filled containers on their heads. They stayed close to Kakembo as he guided the heavily loaded bike down an extremely muddy and bumpy path.

This water, even though murky, was necessary for bathing, cooking, and laundry. Purified water to drink was essential, but it cost money, and there were no sinks or plumbing at the orphanage.

"What an enormous task this must have been without having a bike," I thought to myself. Even with the bike, it was a lot of work, still requiring a long walk back and forth from the orphanage. Yet Kakembo took it all in stride!

In my reading about Uganda, I learned most people walk in the rural areas. However, incredulous balancing acts of people or heavy loads of materials on bicycles and motorcycles, or boda bodas (motorcycle taxis), are not uncommon!

According to Wikipedia, Mityana is town of about 95,000 people, has many rural villages surrounding it. Kampala, about forty miles away and with a population of about 1.6 million people, is terribly congested with chaotic traffic, people, and shops. Kakembo occasionally needs to travel there by bus for certain items. On his return, he has expressed his feelings of being absolutely frazzled and stressed. It renews his appreciation to the slower way of life in Mityana with its outlying hills and mountains.

"Am going to be praying and fasting in order to thank the Lord for all He has done for us," Kakembo reported. "We are so grateful . . . baby Moses was able to get out of the bad situation because of the Lord. And we are also able to get the means of transport . . . am going to be thanking and putting my knees down for His glory. And Mom, I now have a bicycle to visit the prayer mountain so I can reach in time and also come back in time!" His sweet words meant so much to me.

I noticed Bob was scrutinizing the photos I shared with him of the children drawing water and carrying the heavy containers. He began to whisper to himself, "I wonder . . ." His words became audible.

"They get a lot of rain there, don't they? What if gutters were put up to collect the rain water in a large barrel?" He did a web search to see how much rain Mityana received. Then he calculated square inches of roof, length of gutters, and other calculations. I had no idea what he was doing!

"You know!" Bob said excitedly. "They would get enough rain to fill a good-sized container! And they could put a spigot on the barrel and at least have enough water to wash and clean!"

"Wow, honey! That's a terrific idea! Wonderful idea! Let me run that by Kakembo," I replied, excited by the plan. Maybe we could actually help in an even more significant way than previously thought in this difficult water situation!

And so we did! Kakembo went through a good deal of research. Within weeks, he had a cement foundation put in and placed a 10,000 liter barrel on it, complete with spigots. The installed gutters channeled the seasonal abundant rain waters into the large tank. It was perfect timing as the rainy season was just beginning!

A verse came to my mind, "Give, and it will be given to you: A good measure, pressed down, shaken together, and running over will be poured into your lap. For with the same measure you use, it will be measured to you" (Luke 6:38). I definitely felt I was receiving an abundant good measure of God-sent love and joy running over in my heart!

Kakembo later enthusiastically reported that the installed water tank made it far easier for cleaning and bathing, especially with thirty-three dirt-loving kids! The photo certainly attested to that as the children appeared clean and happy! "Am dreaming big next year, in Jesus's mighty name, that we can collect and sell some of the water, and we save and buy a small plot of land to plant crops. My dream is one day we can be self-supporting!"

Oh, dear Kakembo, dream big, dream big, dear mutabani! We were beginning to dream as well about that possibility!

PROPERTY & PRAYER

THE SOUND OF Kakembo's message woke me up with the familiar sound. "Good morning, dear Mom, oli otya? [how are you?] ... was told there is a man in our community that is having problems. He is selling his plot of land at a cheaper price ... we can take that opportunity and talk with him and bargain ... if there is no money, we can rent a plot of land to farm on ... how do you see, Mom?"

His style of English was appealing to me. Britain had ruled in Uganda until 1962, and occasionally I denoted that hint of British influence. However, accent or not, I was surprised at his request of buying land coming so quickly!

"Land? Well we are talking a significant sum of money here, no doubt!" I thought to myself. I shared the message with Bob, and I was very surprised at his openness to the idea.

We both wanted the orphanage to become more self-sustaining. It was beginning to seem that the Lord was connecting Bob and my heart together to these beloved kids and caregivers! I told Kakembo we were making no promises, but I asked that he at least inquire more about it and give it some time.

"This man has a sick child, and he is also being demanded . . . he is having too much debt, so he is selling his plot of land at a cheaper price . . . this is really a chance for us, Mom! His child is suffering from a serious heart disease, so he needs the money so he can save his son's life," Kakembo went on. I loved his foresight and caring nature.

I took a deep breath and asked the most important question in my mind at that moment, "And . . . so . . . what is the price of the land?"

Kakembo revealed he had been successful at bargaining the price down. The land was very inexpensive compared to what land would cost in our area of Idaho. There was even an irrigation stream running through it with some remains of a previous crop. The land was about four miles from the orphanage. There was just one caveat. "He needs the money immediately to save his son, Mom," Kakembo added. Sigh, it seemed medical emergencies were such a part of life there!

Bob and I looked at each other, hesitated, then took time to pray and inquire of God. It really was only minutes before we both had a confirmation in our hearts.

We knew this was indeed a wonderful opportunity we could not pass up for the orphanage, nor could we ignore the medical need. Not only would we be helping this father, but the opportunity also lent itself toward our key goal of helping the orphanage to become self-sustaining. Little did we know, however, how important this plot of land would later become!

Kakembo's excitement showed in his reply, "Wow this is great news! I can't believe this . . . thank you thank you so much . . . this is a miracle indeed! Oh, the Lord is really great!"

"It's wonderful to be part of your miracle," I answered. And it truly was! "I went back and talked to the man," Kakembo continued. "I told him we are going to buy the land, and he was so happy to hear the good news."

Bob asked me to remind Kakembo to ask the man if he could pray over his son. "I've already done that, Mom," he replied. "I also told the father about the power of Jesus Christ and what He has done for me . . . that I am a walking miracle! He told me he wants to become born again, and I converted him to the Lord."

Wow! It seemed that our investment already was bearing fruit, spiritual fruit, through this dear son in Christ! We became so grateful that the Lord had led us to this heart-to-heart connection with Kakembo and the orphanage.

The subsequent week, however, could have used another miracle or two on my end! I learned again—the hard way. Transferring funds via Western Union set off a fraud alert as I sent what they considered too large an amount to Uganda. Apparently, fraud is rampant in Africa, along with dark money going to terrorists, and Western Union was taking no chances. I began doing a series of corrections that only delayed the needed funds! It gave me a very unpleasant feeling of déjà vu all over again!

"What are we going to do, Mom? Am worried. The boy may die . . . I talked to the man, and he told me surgery is in three days . . .

he is confused and desperate!" Kakembo relayed. "I will be fasting tomorrow at the prayer mountain for the young boy."

I had to resort once again to send the funds via the much slower bank transfer method. I expressed my fear about the frustrating delay to Kakembo. Yet he remained full of faith. "I do believe the transaction reaches here in time . . . am also praying hard for the boy . . . don't worry, Mom," he reassured me, but worry I did.

The next morning I was pleasantly surprised to read, "The good news here is the money you sent has arrived . . . am so happy right now, Mom!"

"Oh, you of little faith," I said to myself. I was thrilled!

"First thing tomorrow, am going to see the man, Mr. Mutyaba, and we start processing on agreements and other land titles. We need to act fast and see that the boy starts on his treatment . . ."

"I will do all in my power to see that my kids get a better world ahead of them . . . a permanent home and now a way to grow food . . ." He continued, "You became our friend, our sister, role model, mentor, and above all, our mother in Christ. I am so exhausted right now. I have worked so hard today . . . we send our love to you, Mom, and Dad Bob. Thank you, thank you, and Dad Bob so much! We love you dearly and forever."

Kakembo's engaging and very grateful words humbled me, but I rejoiced in reading them. I rolled over to sleep with a big smile on my face that night.

The next morning I read, "I forgot to tell you that Mr. Mutyaba said today is the day his son is getting surgery . . . I will be climbing the prayer mountain today for his life. Am going to join hands with Joseph for the safety of the boy. Is there anything, Mom, you need me to pray for?" This was a frequent question he asked me when he would go to his prayer mountain.

"Hello, dear Mom, the boy got his surgery, but we need prayers . . . his situation is critical." I read Kakembo's words with concern. Bob and I so wanted the boy to have a successful surgery as a testimony to this man with his newly found faith in Jesus! And we did believe the Lord would provide that.

Kakembo's later words were startling, and a deep feeling of sadness came over me. "I really have bad news, Mom. The boy passed away today . . . he was only thirteen. It's night here, but am still at the house of the father. I feel down, Mom. I will stay by his side and comfort him in Jesus Christ."

I reminded Kakembo of the words in Psalm 56:8, "You have kept record of my days of wandering. You have stored my tears in your bottle, and counted each of them" (Contemporary English Version).

"Oh, I will read this verse for him because he is in deep sorrow . . . I think I also have a chance to preach the Word of God cause there are other family members all gathered here." Kakembo used the opportunity to share Christ. His heart was connected closely to the Lord. He was an evangelist at heart.

I assured Kakembo that we were praying for him during that opportunity the Lord had given him. He reminded me, "I promised the

Lord when I was down in bed before my surgery . . . I promised Him that if he made me through, I will serve Him with all my heart." His words were so precious to me.

"I love your heart," I answered. Indeed I had come to love that very heart deeply, a heart devoted intensely to the Lord and the children he loves and cares for.

FAITH & CULTIVATION

PHOTOS OF THE land were exciting to see! There was so much potential for growing vegetables and even banana trees. I asked how they would protect the produce from people who might steal them. Kakembo told me it wasn't the people we needed to worry about; it was the monkeys! But at that point, monkeys weren't our main concern. Tilling the land and planting corn, beans, ground nuts (peanuts), cabbage, and bananas would come first. The previous remains of a prior crop were all in very bad condition. The land needed tilling and replanting.

I wasn't anticipating the high costs for renting a tractor and buying the specialized seeds and fertilizer for that type of soil; this, along with extra tools, as needed. Our pockets were still burning from the purchase of the land. I began to grumble. "Lord, we could use a little help here, please!" I prayed as I walked to the mailbox.

I had forgotten about a conversation I had with a dear friend, Susan, in Anchorage, Alaska. She and her husband, Dennis, were interested in the orphanage. Susan had followed my Facebook posts.

I noticed her letter in the mailbox. As I opened it, I gasped in unbelief! Along with her note was a very generous check she had sent me for the orphanage. The Lord had provided through these dear friends! As Kakembo gratefully reminded me, it was a miracle!

Indeed it was, and this time I was on the recipient end as well! As Susan said, "Kind of reminds me of an old song. If I never had a problem, I would never know that God could solve them. I wouldn't know what faith in God can do!"

Those funds were used in the rental of a tractor, the seeds, plants, fertilizers, and supplies. And enough money was left toward the remaining needs to feed the children that month. God is good! Before long, the garden would begin to supply for those food needs.

It was 10:30 p.m. my time, but I was pleased to read that there was sunshine in the Mityana area. "It's morning here . . . am already in the garden with my kids," Kakembo messaged while sending photos of the kids working in the dirt. I laughed, "Ha! It looks like the kids are having fun! You'll have a lot of baths tonight!"

"They love playing in the garden field, and I enjoy seeing them happy. They have been removing grass and stones. We have just planted beans," he replied. Then there would be the planting of corn, peanuts, cabbage, and some banana trees. It was later I learned that the corn would be dried and taken to a grinder to make corn meal. The corn kernels and cobs were ground to use for breakfast mush.

"Did the kids walk the four miles?" I asked.

"We use our bicycle to take some, and we come back, to pick up others," he wrote. I was thinking to myself that it must have been a lot of bike riding! How did they have any energy left for garden work?

The children were a bundle of vitality and fun, but they would grow up to be a hardworking crew for future crops. Their tutors would ensure that!

Preacher Teacher

THE SMALL CHURCH started by Pastor Ssemwogelere was required to abandon the rented building during the pandemic. They currently meet in a very simple chapel structure made of wood and aluminum with a platform for the altar on land owned by the pastor. The few church members are praying they can improve on the construction in the future.

Small gatherings in churches are slowly beginning to open up again after the COVID-19 pandemic. Little by little, a few more people are attending, and Kakembo tells me of his opportunities to preach. I love to see his excitement as he serves the Lord.

On some Sundays, after Joseph, Brenda, and Kakembo have fed, cleaned, and dressed the children, they would take them all to church. It was an instant congregation!

I smiled as I watched the video clip Kakembo sent me. He was preaching and began in his appealing accent. "I am bringing this word to you from our Lord Jesus Christ. In Mark 10, it says they were bringing children to Him so that they might touch him. But the disciples rebuked them. But Jesus became indignant and said, 'Permit the children to come to Me, do not hinder them!'"

The video panned out, and I saw some of the kids squirming on their wooden benches. I also heard Joseph's voice gently scold them for giggling.

As Kakembo began to preach in his native language, his voice became louder and quickened in pace. Almost instantly, those squirmy kids became attentive. Each pair of eyes appeared to now be glued on their beloved pastor as they listened to his every word. I was certain Pastor Ssemwogelere influenced Kakembo's love for preaching.

Kakembo had engaged their interest. As he made a final statement, the kids raised their arms, some standing to their feet, chanting, "Amina! Amina!" They were clearly involved, affirming his words with their loud amens! It was gratifying to see these young minds and hearts passionately connecting with their dear pastor/teacher's words.

"I have to go and help bathe the kids, Mom," Kakembo says to me frequently in our evening conversations. There would also be prayer time and tucking them in. Brenda, Joseph, and perhaps some of the older children would help. Nevertheless, the nightly routine has to be quite an undertaking with so many kids!

Even though sleeping conditions were meager, I witnessed this devoted team's love and care. Kakembo signed off that night, saying, "Have a good night, Mom, and Dad Bob too. We love you . . . may the Lord give you everything you need in life and good health so that you will see these kids becoming responsible men and women in our community!" I loved the deep sense of pride and passion for the children that he embraced.

I have since learned that the children do not have beds. They sleep on homemade mats that the women in the community have made. It made me realize how important those blankets were that we had given earlier. Those floors had to be cold! It is another future dream, perhaps, beds, or at the least mattresses, for all the children and adults!

I read that in parts of Africa, parents assign their children with both first and last names. It's not unusual for families to have children with different last names in these particular areas. Since the orphanage children have no parents, Pastor Ssemwogelere gave their names to them. Being found on the streets leaves these orphans without an identity, so belonging to a family is very important. The orphanage has not only given them names, they have been given an identity in Christ and nurturing of love and care through these humble caregivers. Together they are bound by Christ's love, and together they belong to the family of God.

Christmas Provisions

"**How was your** day?" I asked Kakembo.

"Good cause we did some cleaning at the orphanage. And the Lord gave us rain water for the provision!" Kakembo answered.

It was getting close to Christmas. I thought how good it was that the tank provided the water needed for the clean-up time. The long trip to the murky streams would have left them so tired! This way, the children had enough energy for mopping and doing other errands. They worked together as a team.

In America, we take for granted so many of the small necessities of life. I discovered the children had no toothbrushes or toothpaste. Kakembo reminded me that such items weren't considered necessities when the first priority is food. They used charcoal, salt, and sticks. I thought that odd at first, but then, it explained to me why toothpaste in the US is now available with a charcoal ingredient! Perhaps Uganda had the secret for white teeth even before we did!

I had previously asked Kakembo if he had ever tasted pizza. His reply, "No Mom, I have never tasted it. Pizza is something for the rich here." He then asked me if I had ever eaten grasshoppers.

"No way!" I answered. "You roast them, Mom, and they are yummy!"

"I'm not too sure about that," I told him. "They'd have to be decapitated, gutted, and burned to a crisp before I'd eat those things!" He laughed.

Kakembo's tender words that morning didn't surprise me: "I would like to give back to the elderly, disabled, and girls in our community on the birthday of our Lord Jesus, Mom." This was a Christmas wish he had. Later, he shared that he wanted to buy the two adolescent girls in the orphanage pads for their monthly cycle as they would otherwise skip school during those weeks.

Not many young men in this world at his age would even be attentive to the needs of teenage girls! He is a unique and incredibly sensitive Christian leader seizing the opportunity to supply the needs of even his young adolescent girls.

Christmas was coming up, and we wanted to ensure that Christmas dinner would be special this year. Meat would be on the menu! Kakembo explained, "We also have to buy the beans and posho, which we are going to be fed before Christmas. We buy the chicken when it's still alive, and we keep it alive up to Christmas," Kakembo went on.

"So you butcher and pluck the chickens too?" I asked incredulously.

"Yes, hahaha, with the kids. We killed chickens once before, so they now know how, but some have fear."

"I can imagine! I would be afraid too!" I replied.

"Oh, it means you fear too, Mom?"

"Yes! I would have LOTS of fear too," I chuckled.

I couldn't imagine the children witnessing a headless chicken with blood squirting out the top and frantically running in circles in the midst of them! But from our conversation, it sounded like it would have been me who would have been traumatized while looking on in horror and not so much the children!

In the end, I convinced him that it would be too much of an ordeal! He agreed to buy pre-butchered chickens and some meat for the Christmas feast.

We planned together to make Christmas special for the children. Bob and I were able to provide enough funds for Kakembo to buy a small clothing item for each child and some toys to share.

The Christmas feast would be delicious as the meat-based soup would be poured over the rice. All of this would be made over a fire pit.

There would be music and dancing, and Bob and I made a Christmas video for the kids in our Christmas hats.

I couldn't wait to see their photos. And they did not disappoint!

I especially loved the video Kakembo shared of a dear eighty-two-year-old widow he had invited to the Christmas celebration. She enchanted me as I watched her sway and dance to the lively, rhythmic Ugandan music, swirling in her flowing dress of layered purple and pink.

I was captivated by this beautiful elderly African woman, and I could hear Kakembo's gentle laugh, which I loved, as he encouraged this gracefully aged woman to dance on! What pure joy!

Football, Fasting, & Plucked Chickens

"DID YOU HAVE a good day yesterday, son?" I asked "Oh yes, Mom, although it rained here. But we had a match of football in our community to improve the life of girls. Everyone who came had to pay some, and the players had to pay. The money was collected to buy pads and other girl necessities. I was very happy and blessed that I was part of it. It was one of my prayers to contribute to the girls' needs in our community during this season."

"That was so nice for the community to do that! Did you play?"

"Yes, haha, I even scored a goal!" he replied.

"I would have loved to have been there to see you play!"

"Haha! You would have been proud!" He went on to describe that everyone was shouting loudly and cheering him on. They were yelling excitedly, "Go, Pastor!" as he ran the field and kicked the ball into the goal. He added, "I feel happy for being part of the well-being of others and contributing the little I have to others who don't."

I explained to Kakembo that we call their game soccer in the US. We play a different game that is called football. I sent him a text photo of a football.

"Oh my, is that even football? It seems like an oval-shaped ball . . . is it for the foot?"

"Yes, and they hold the ball vertically and kick it," I laughed.

"Hahaha . . . I have never seen something like that . . . woo! Maybe when you can come to visit sometime, you will have to teach us American football. Haha! I believe we could make a good team with you, Mom, as our coach!"

I laughed loudly at the thought: a sixty-eight-year-old white American woman running and stumbling pathetically out there on the field with these two strong, agile, and athletic African men! Their animated and excited kids would complete the team. What a sight that would be!

"Was Joseph able to go?" I asked. Joseph had been down with malaria, a common illness due to the many mosquitos in the humid environment. After several weeks with proper medicine and treatments, he was doing much better.

"Yes, Mom; he was shouting so loud every time I was with the ball! His voice even changed."

I giggled as I explained to Kakembo that we would say, "he lost his voice" in the US. "I would have been screaming even louder and would have lost my voice too if I would have been there!" I chuckled.

"Yes, Joseph lost his voice," he replied, "and I can't stop laughing at the way he is talking now!"

Hearing these two brothers enjoying themselves did my heart good! To be able to get the community together in a game of soccer was absolutely wonderful after two long years of miserable COVID-19 lockdowns. The community loved being together again, every minute of it! What a blessing!

Hi son, how are you doing?" I greeted. "I'm doing fine, Mom . . . praising God for his mercies that never end!" We chatted for a while, and I mentioned that I shouldn't keep him away from breakfast. He commented, "No problem . . . I'm fasting, so no worries!" I affirmed with him that this was an important spiritual resource in our walk with the Lord.

At the same time, I was thinking how lean he was already, and how he could benefit with more meals under his belt!

Sometimes as I read the news headlines: war, the dangers of the US becoming a socialist nation, COVID-19, crime-ridden cities with savage killings, corruption of government, elections, the Delta and Omicron variants, and on and on, I cannot help but to turn my eyes away, choosing to think about the beautiful love of this precious orphanage!

The Lord's ways are more evident as I observe these three young adults depending so entirely on His mercy, grace, and Word in their daily tasks. What a contrast to the terrors and chaos of the world with no hope!

Yes, there is sickness, sorrow, poverty, suffering, and disappointment in the world and the orphanage. However, the sufferings they have endured have been interwoven with the authentic and divine love of our Lord and Savior. And in this process, I'm finding that the Lord is purifying, sanctifying, and dwelling in their hearts. He is also sanctifying Bob and my hearts while weaving our hearts with theirs in His divine love and purpose.

As I was meditating on how we could better assist with the orphanage needs, an idea came to me.

"Chickens! That's what the orphanage needs!" I emphatically said to myself. "They'll have a constant supply of eggs that way! Maybe they'll eventually have enough to sell." Bob agreed the idea was a good one.

Of course, Kakembo loved the idea! Again, it was another small step to becoming hunger immune. Inflation was hitting Uganda just as badly as the US, so this good source of protein for the kids would be perfect for their ever-growing bodies. Kakembo would see to getting a chicken coop built and order the live chickens.

The day finally arrived when the shipment came in, and they could pick the hens up, along with some broilers. The roosters would come later.

His photos left me no doubt that the children were tickled pink and loved holding them! It would be a fun adventure for them to discover and collect freshly-laid eggs in the future. The day of butchering and plucking, however, would be another story entirely!

Eviction Chaos

It was early January, 2022, and it had been several days that I hadn't heard from Kakembo. I thought it was probably a network connection problem like times before. But after three days, and no answer to my question as to how he was doing, I became a bit concerned. The next day, I was relieved to hear the familiar "ding" of Messenger.

"Hello, Mom, am not well. I have been admitted in the hospital.

"In the hospital?" I exclaimed. "Why?"

"Yes, Mom. I fainted after the chairman of our community gave me the news that our orphanage land and building was sold!" was his reply.

I couldn't believe what Kakembo's message was saying. I read his message again. "That can't be happening!" I told myself. He went on to explain that the unexpected and abrupt news of this sudden eviction shocked him to the core so much so that he literally passed out in the chairman's office, hitting his head on a concrete floor. He was then taken to the hospital.

Kakembo had told me previous times that Pastor Ssemwogelere had been given the property by a gentleman in the community, and the orphanage had remained there for some years. Kakembo and Joseph had been assured by the pastor that the building and land would eventually be given to them when it came his time to leave this earth.

However, there was no formal land title documents in the original transaction. It was done verbally in the presence of witnesses, which was common in those days. There was no question in Pastor Ssemwogelere's mind that the building and land belonged to him.

Nevertheless, the original owner who had given the property to the pastor had died in the recent weeks. His relatives sold the property in the interim without notice. Needless to say, the news shocked the pastor!

Evictions are becoming commonplace in Uganda for farmers, in particular. Land has been taken away, paving the way for development, and a more recent development of drilling for oil has involved illegal evictions of landowners. In addition, North Africa has a large Islamic population, and they have purchasing power for buying many properties in Africa.

Kakembo explained that as soon as he was treated at the hospital, he and Joseph ran back to the commissioner's office. They both fell on their knees, begging this new owner to consider the needs of the thirty-three orphans as they had absolutely nowhere to go!

Kakembo described the scene. "They didn't want to hear from us, the poor. What hurts me most is that they knew the land they are buying is occupied with poor orphans, but they went ahead to do so anyway! I was crying to them on my knees with my brother, but they told us to leave."

I learned later this new owner was antagonistic toward Christians. He actually called Kakembo and Joseph "dogs" and shouted to them, "Where is your God now?" as the two brothers exited out the door. Proverbs 18:23 was so true in this case, "A poor man pleads for mercy, but a rich man answers harshly."

Hearing that made my blood boil! I would have been so angry to that man's face! Kakembo's response, however, was 180 degrees opposite than mine! He went on to say, "That's why I cried all night to God to help me forgive him for what he has done to these, God's children."

I reminded Kakembo that he is a son of Almighty God. He reaffirmed, saying, "I am a son of the Most High, and no matter what I am going through, I am not ashamed of my Lord God!" Despite the cruel treatment of this new owner, Kakembo prayed he could forgive him.

He went on, "At least we own the land you gave us with proper documents, and no one can steal it from us!" We had insisted on formal documents when the land was purchased. "Hmm," I began to wonder. "Perhaps there may be more to God's leading us to purchase the land than I previously thought!" His ways are beyond our ways!

Brenda was crushed from hearing the news. "Right now Brenda is so lost in thoughts. Yesterday she was crying all day and telling me she is so worried about the kids."

Overwhelming fears rose in their hearts, as well as the hearts of the children. Where would they go? What would happen to them? How would they live? Would they all be separated? Would they be forced back onto the streets all over again? Those same thoughts began to haunt me into the night as well.

After serious discussion, Bob and I agreed, and we assured Kakembo that we would help in any and all ways we could. The last thing we would allow was the separation of the children from their loving caregivers! They were knit in their hearts as brothers and sisters, mother and fathers. They had become dear to us, but I knew that God would have to do some miraculous working on His part!

The town commissioner advised Kakembo and Joseph to take it to their village court. Perhaps they would be granted some extra time to move out. But where would they go?

Kakembo was suffering with severe headaches, no doubt from a mild concussion. He stated that the court hearing would be his following day at 11:30 a.m., which would be at 1:30 a.m. my time. I was happy it was set to be heard so soon. Bob and I would be praying very hard!

Kakembo informed me the following morning that he was up most of the night praying. I gave him a verse, Isaiah 41:10: "Do not fear for I am with you. Do not be dismayed, for I am your God. I will strengthen you; I will uphold you with My righteous right hand." "That verse is for you son," I said.

"Oh what a wonderful word from our Lord," he replied. "Am so grateful . . . these words are my pillars!" I was learning that this dear young man loved the Word of God!

The morning of the hearing had arrived, and due to the time difference, the hearing had been completed by my morning wake-up. I immediately messaged, asking for any news.

"Glory to the Lord, Mom! The court has granted us five months before we have to leave!" he jubilantly reported. "And the judge seriously warned the new landowners from threatening us!"

"Did many community members show up?" I asked. "Yes, Mom, and for some, they had to beg the judge for not taking them to jail," was his strange reply.

He explained that the community people were so angry with this new owner that they began to make threats against him for heartlessly forcing the orphanage out. The new owner was throwing threats back as well. The judge then had to come down hard, threatening jail sentences to them all! The court session had become a hotbed of angry emotions.

Community members believed the orphanage should have been the rightful owner and that this new owner with money had no heart whatsoever. They, no doubt, were morally right in their deep feelings, yet money talked, and the new owner had money!

The Saturday following, I asked, "Hello, son, how was your Sunday?"

"Sunday was full of love as we met. We had people from the community there wishing us well." I asked him what he preached on. "I preached about anger," Kakembo replied.

"Well, you had plenty of examples of that at the court hearing!" I joked.

"Yes, I preached on James 1:20, that "the anger of man does not produce the righteousness of God.""

The thought hit me at how bold he was to preach on a topic that was still so close to their hearts. The emotions, no doubt, were still running high, and I wondered if this new owner would ever fit into the community. But if it was up to Kakembo, he would allow the Lord to work on forgiving him.

The news of allowing five months for moving out of the present orphanage was good news, for sure. But at the same time, Bob and I were somewhat stunned at the prospect of a building project to house all thirty-three of those children! They would have to be out of the current building by the end of May, and we had mutually agreed we would back the orphanage in any way we could.

Now it meant getting a building built on the garden land we had previously purchased. It had become obvious to us that God had this in mind all along, and it was no surprise to Him! He was in control! But it was a definite and unexpected turn of events for us! We were learning that we were just willing vessels to carry out His plan in what seemed to be uncharted waters ahead.

In the meantime, I was reading news story after news story of the imminent danger of war with Russia. The stock market had been hit with a 1000-point decline, among many recent declines, and our retirement savings were taking big hits. Inflation was rising steeply, yet our inner conviction grew about the need to house these precious children as soon as possible!

"Wow Lord, give me your faith for this new adventure," I asked.

Sometimes I felt like I was on a rollercoaster barreling down an exhilarating chute and waving my raised arms high while shouting "whee" all the way down! Other times, I was crying out, "Lord! Help! What in the world are we doing?"

It worried me as I read a headline in the Uganda Monitor news site that morning, "30,000 evicted locals cry to government for compensation." Corruption is rampant in Uganda, unfortunately, as it is in so many places in our world, including the US! In addition to this, news of the huge increase of construction costs was in the Uganda headlines. In some places, cement was being rationed. Brick prices as well as nails were beginning to rise steadily!

Isaiah 26:3,4 says, "You will keep in perfect peace those whose minds are stayed on You, because they trust in You." If ever I needed to keep my mind stayed on Him and not on the news, it was now!

The world was beginning to feel like a very insecure and perilous place, and the commitment we had made to the orphanage felt precarious as well. Yet Kakembo marched on in faith, believing the Lord was with him every step of the way, giving God the glory! We, on the other hand, just tried to keep up and stay in step with his faith-filled vision!

CLEARING THE PLOT

"HELLO, MOM, I wanted to inform you that the children have not started school yet as they are of great importance at the garden cause we have been picking corn today," Kakembo reported.

School had finally opened after many long months of COVID-19 closures. He let me know the kids were not one bit excited in the least, however, about the educational opportunities that awaited them the following week. They were children after all, and spending the days running in the garden, digging in the dirt, and picking corn was their hearts' delight! It was his intention to harvest the corn, cabbage, and peanuts and then dig up that area for the building site.

"Concerning the building, the chairman donated twenty bags of cement, the school donated sand, and I have enough funds for starting the blocks," he reassured me. Comforted by his words, I knew that, nevertheless, there would be loads of more materials required!

The initial task would be clearing the building site. The men from the community would help them out with that huge struggle. After that, the building project itself would be the enormous undertaking.

I was astonished at the video of a massive stump being removed. I watched the men cautiously rocking the huge, entrenched root back and forth.

Eventually, it gave way with a loud crack, and the guys laughed victoriously as they proudly stared at the results of their physical achievement.

"The chairman has spent the whole day with us in the garden, saying we need to be quick about building," Kakembo remarked. And fast it did go! The following week, rooms were being quartered in the roped area, and soon a foundation of bricks emerged, with ongoing photos showing them rising higher and higher each day!

It was a dream coming true for Brenda, Joseph, and Kakembo! They would now truly have a forever home on their forever land, with proper title documents! No one could ever again send them away to the streets!

The orphanage was awakening to the precious promise given in Jeremiah 29:11, "'For I know the plans I have for you,' declares the Lord, 'plans to prosper you and not to harm you, plans to give to give you hope and a future,'" as well as Romans 8:28, "And we know that in all things God works for the good of those who love Him, who have been called according to His purpose."

HEART ISSUES

"**HOW WAS YOUR** day, my mountain Mama?" Kakembo greeted me later that week.

"Very fine, son. I am getting ready for my twin sister, Vickie, to visit. I'm looking forward to it, and she'll be staying with us for about a week," I answered.

Kakembo knew well about a tightly-knit sibling affection through his younger brother, Joseph. They were, in essence, best friends and true brothers, as well as brothers in Christ!

Vickie and I grew up with close emotional ties as well. Yearning for best friends was not a problem in our growing years as we tended to meet those longings through our close twin-sister connection that started at birth. However, there was a time in our senior year when that close kinship was severed rather abruptly.

Vickie had found a new and earnest faith in the Lord Jesus just prior to our graduation from high school. Her faith in Christ became life-changing for her. It was an abrupt ending, however, to our wild senior year of dating, partying, and the heartfelt ties we had once enjoyed. It seemed as if an invisible barrier came between us.

Try as I might, I could not seem to talk any sense into this somehow newly "sainted" representation of what was formerly my fun-loving twin sister. Any and all discussions I had with her were met with a strange and foreign "heavenly" frame of mind as Vickie shared her newfound faith with me. I thought she had literally gone nuts!

Everything familiar about Vickie was not so slowly changing before my eyes: the way she dressed, her change of makeup, her disinterest in partying, her new obsession with the Bible, her Bible studies and worship with the "Jesus People," and on and on! And then, of all things, she became interested in becoming a missionary! I thought she had lost it!

I would never have dreamed then that the Lord would indeed one day lead my dear sister into a career as a missionary! Yet the Lord God had His plans, and her newly married husband, Alan Foster, would even take her as far as the primitive jungles of Bolivia, reaching lost tribes for Christ!

In a final act of desperation, I sat down with her for a heart-to-heart talk to bring her back to her senses. I meant business, serious business, about this ridiculously inflated spiritual infatuation she was going through. Yet, in a serious twist of fate, it was me who would change.

During this desperate discussion, I actually listened to her words, or should I say, to the Lord's voice for the very first time. She talked of the Lord Jesus as her newly found Master, Savior, and deepest friend. I had never heard such things!

Little by little, it was as if the wax ear plugs began dissolving from my spiritual ears, and the eye cataracts began to disappear from my spiritual eyes. My dear twin was being used to open my eyes to the divine love and nature of the Lord Jesus Christ. She revealed to me that our Lord greatly desires to have a personal relationship with each one of us.

It wasn't long after that I, too, invited Him into my heart and life as Lord and Savior. I, too, became increasingly hungry to learn more about this newly found adventure with the Lord at the helm. I, too, became hungry to read His words and grow spiritually.

My life, as well as my sister's, have never been the same since that day some fifty-one years ago!

I had shared my testimony to Kakembo, and I asked him when he first came to know Christ. His answer enlightened me as he explained that for him, as an orphan, it was not at all difficult to come to the Lord.

He was just a poor orphan as a youngster, and who else but the God of the universe could help him? There was no other Hope and no other way! He was not blinded as many are in our prosperous nation to the desperate need for God to save him! It came almost naturally to him to reach out to the only one who could!

How different it can be with the prosperous. We make our own ways, proudly, independently, and with our own self-reliance, separating ourselves from God and His ways. Could it be there will be many many more of the poor in the kingdom of God than of the prosperous? As Jesus once indicated, "It is easier for a camel to go through the eye of a needle than for someone who is rich to enter the Kingdom of God" (Matt. 19:24). How encouraging it is that He added Matthew 19:26, "With man this is impossible, but with God all things are possible!"

It seemed now the Lord was leading in a new chapter for the orphanage. I truly felt privileged that the Lord included Bob and me in His plans!

"How was your night, Mom?" Kakembo asked.

I grumbled in jest, "I didn't get much sleep last night due to Bob's snoring!"

"Oh no! Does Dad Bob snore? Hahaha, I think it was that he was just too tired," Kakembo replied.

"Yes, he snores, and very loudly!" I lamented.

Kakembo mentioned, "The kids snore here every night. Some talk in their sleep, while others even shout aloud while sleeping!"

No doubt the orphanage children were acting out their day in their sleep, but I wondered if some were still dealing with the traumas of becoming orphans. Surely there had to be many ingrained fears from their feelings of vulnerability, loss, and hopelessness. Some, like Kakembo, had witnessed a parent dying.

Brenda, Joseph, and Kakembo knew and understood those deeply ingrained feelings. The tender care and compassion that these loving caregivers give the children help draw these little ones to feel safe and very loved. The orphanage is their home, and they would learn about the protection and love of the Lord as their spiritual foundation.

The schools had opened again in Uganda, and there was much for the children to catch up due to the two-year closure due to COVID-19. Kakembo informed me that the children start their school day at 6:30 in the morning and end at 6:30 at night after a meal, bathing, and prayers. The walk to school is long, yet during that time, the children are bonding with their caregivers as they discuss their school days and, no doubt, spiritual lessons to be learned.

Joseph walked the kids to school while Kakembo supervised the building site. It was a long walk, but as Kakembo said, "Joseph walks them while they sing gospel songs until they reach the school." However, coming back from school leaves them very tired after eight hours of study. That means a quick supper and right to bed!

On the other hand, there is no singing while walking during cool rainy days, and the kids arrive soaking wet! And with a full day of school and a long walk back, many of the children come back to the orphanage exhausted and shivering from the cold. What I would do to buy a van for them! But a building was in process, so transportation was out of the picture for now. However, buying raincoats for the rainy season would have to be a purchase item for sure!

"Please pray for me, Mom," was Kakembo's evening request.

"Oh dear, what is it?" I asked.

Kakembo went on to explain. "I have been having so much on my mind, and I think I have been struggling too much using my body and not my soul. I have been working so hard and am having temper, and I don't know why. May the Lord forgive me."

I empathized with him and reminded him he was likely exhausted from all the physical labor he was doing at the building site, working day in and day out. Along with that was all the care and supervision he needed to give at the orphanage. He had many heavy concerns on his shoulders for such a young man.

His further explanation revealed the root of his frustration as he said, "The new owners of the building have been threatening our kids. They told some of the kids that if we don't leave the land immediately, they will start hurting them! I went and stood up to them and really showed my anger, and they left."

I assured Kakembo that he was right to feel this way, that it was righteous indignation he was feeling at the harassment and threats of these new owners! We agreed to spend time praying about the situation. Afterward, he shared that he felt his soul felt free again.

The following Sunday, I asked Kakembo what he preached on. He replied, "I preached about forgiveness. Romans 12:17 says, 'Do not repay anyone evil for evil.' This verse tells us to give thought to do what is honorable in the sight of everyone." Surely the Lord was guiding Kakembo's heart in His direction.

Up She Rises!

"How is the building going?" I asked one morning. The house plans actually looked quite elaborate, and this process would be a whole new experience for Kakembo! He would have to rely on the builders.

He explained the process. "They are going to be reaching on the beam level within a few days. This beam is made of concrete and beam wires. It's made to strengthen the uppermost part of the roof.

Mom, I also wanted to tell you that they finished digging the outdoor latrine."

I had seen the first photo of the beginning stage of the latrine, but his second photo shocked me! It was twenty-five feet deep! "How does the digger get out?" I asked.

His reply wasn't too reassuring. "He steps on two of the sides as he moves up. It's really risky!" I couldn't imagine how much work it had taken during those hot and muggy days digging in that clay soil and with such a precarious way of entering and exiting! Nevertheless, Kakembo assured me the worker was extremely grateful for the very modest wages he earned for his incredibly difficult and risky work.

Each subsequent series of photos showed the layers of bricks going higher and higher. The rudimentary scaffolding looked iffy to me, and that led me to pray for the safety of these hardworking men.

Kakembo was keeping a log of the expenses he texted regularly to me with receipts, and he continually looked for ways to get the best bargains. "I managed to talk with the man that sells timber, and we negotiated on the price. He agreed to supply us an affordable price," he reassured me. "They have started cutting our house timber from the forest," he continued.

"From the forest!?" I asked, astonished. I just assumed they would have lumber yards like we do here in the US. As I talked with him in the following days, he mentioned, "I'm getting exhausted lately as I have to move every day to the forest to see our timber, then back to the site. Yesterday I got in an accident on my bicycle as I was sloping down the hill, and a wild animal quickly crossed the road. I lost control of the bicycle."

"Oh no!" I exclaimed. Kakembo assured me he wasn't hurt badly, but he certainly got "skinned up!"

"I had no idea you would have to wait for someone to first cut down trees!" I responded.

"Yes, Mom," he replied. "It's far away, but yesterday night, they managed to move for us 239 timbers to the site. Now am going to get the roof maker today and talk with him to negotiate a good price on the labor."

Kakembo was doing the job of a construction foreman as he talked with materials men and laborers, negotiating moderate prices at every turn. Not only did the timber need to be cut, but it also had to be sawed and then dried.

The next day, Kakembo greeted me, saying, "Am done taking porridge and am rushing to the site right now."

I mentioned, "Ok son, have a good day . . . and please don't let go of the handle bars!"

He countered with his familiar "hahaha," and laughing face icon, and I chuckled.

As he sent photos of the roof going up, I couldn't help but notice how perilous it was for the young man high on the roof line. It looked like it could be Kakembo himself! "I'm hoping that's not you on top of that roof line!" I asserted.

He sent a note saying, "Hahaha, am not that one, Mom. I fear high buildings!"

It was a good thing he "feared" high buildings, I thought to myself! There was no safety equipment, hard hats, or tie-offs whatsoever in the photos, as Bob pointed out. The construction workers of Uganda lived very dangerously!

"Hello son, how was your Sunday?" I inquired that evening.

"Good, Mom; service went well, by God's grace. I have missed so much our talks since I have been so busy . . . super busy yesterday and today! The roof workers worked Sunday, so I passed by in the evening. I find energy and determination in all I do cause of God's grace." I loved his enthusiasm, resolve, and dedication to the Lord!

I asked how Joseph and Brenda were doing. Kakembo responded, "Joseph is doing so well as he went to preach on the streets, and Brenda is doing well with the orphanage work."

"Way to go Joseph!" I replied, pleased to hear of Joseph's passion to spread the gospel.

I had read where street preaching is not uncommon in Uganda. Some feel called to preach to those who would never set foot in a church. They have a desire to reach those who have never heard the good news of salvation through Jesus Christ. It was certainly the primary method used by our Lord, as well as his disciples after Jesus's resurrection.

Brenda, Joseph, and Kakembo were experiencing the graciousness of God in their lives after an extended time of extreme hardship. It seems spontaneous to them to share with others how they, too, could experience the Lord and His goodness.

It flows naturally to them and makes me wonder why sharing the Lord to others doesn't flow as freely to me or many Christians in my own country. Could it be that the poor and needy people are so numerous in third-world countries that a passing word of hope draws more listeners? Or perhaps the pride we carry in America for fear of what people would think prevents our publicly sharing the good news.

Among other things, we have sadly become a society who is accustomed to shielding ourselves from the world through masks and electronic devices, minimizing public contact. How important it is for believers to train our spiritual ears to hear the prompting of the Holy Spirit when He urges us to talk to someone about Him. There are many who could be open to God and receptive to listen to a message of hope. Brenda, Joseph, and Kakembo are sensitive to discern those opportunities.

I encouraged Kakembo to rest more as he had been going so hard for weeks on end now. He reminded me, "The work will not stop, Mom, as we still have much to do!"

I was truly amazed at how much had been done in the last several months and with much less cost than I would have ever imagined. I was so proud of his managing accomplishments! However, by now, the world news had become increasingly pessimistic about the war that Russia had started in Ukraine.

It was the beginning of March 2022, and the prices continued to go up everywhere, including Uganda. I had read food prices were increasing by 20 percent in that country. "How would the poor people there survive?" I thought to myself. In addition, the value of the dollar was going down, meaning the orphanage received less shillings for every dollar we sent. "Oh Lord, hear our cries for mercy and grace," I prayed.

The cement floors still needed to be finished, and Kakembo's note said, "I am realizing there has been a rise in everything here because there is a price rise in fuel. There is a shortage of cement, and prices are higher . . . am really afraid, Mom, on the way prices are rising!" I assured him that at least we could thank the Lord that the cement used for bricklaying earlier was completed at a much lower cost.

The building was finally beginning to look like a house, not a large one, but a home for the children. But there was a deadline to meet, and indeed the work could not stop to meet that deadline.

When I asked Kakembo how his day went, he answered, "My day was so perfect. Let me show you what made my day so great." His photos surprised me.

"Wow! That roof really sets it apart! I'm so glad we decided to go with the better quality roofing that Dad Bob wanted," I remarked. Having worked with sheet metal, he knew during the rainy season, there would be so much rain that a good roof would be important. There was even enough pieces of roofing left over to give a decent roof to the latrine!

Nevertheless, the house would not have a furnace, kitchen appliances, nor furniture. I suppose having thirty-six people living in approximately1600 square feet would provide enough body heat!

It had been a cold day there, and Kakembo assured me windows, doors, and a couple of lightbulbs would also help to keep the house warmer. He returned back from the site shivering and very cold!

Bars would also be added to doors and windows due to the high level of theft. We talked about plumbing a toilet and shower for the inside, as using the outdoor latrine at night could be dangerous for the kids. Kakembo was delighted at the thought of an indoor toilet, a luxury he had never had before! We decided to include indoor plumbing and showers!

MALARIA, TYPHOID, WAR & SNAKES!

"OH SON, WHAT a darling!" I remarked as I gazed at the photo he sent.

"She didn't go to school today as her cough is too much," he explained.

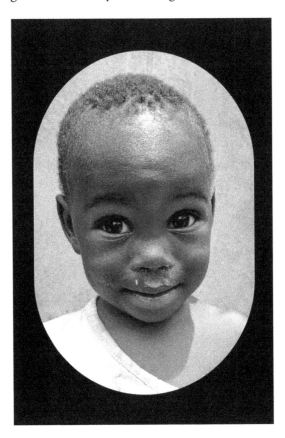

"Oh, poor sweetheart! She has such big eyes!" I beamed. I learned her name was Nakayenga Silvia. It was just a day later that I discovered Kakembo was up a lot at night with several more children who were sick with headaches, chest pains, and coughing.

"Am feeling down, and I don't know why, Mom," he said. I told him it was likely he was just plain worn out and probably catching a cold too, and I encouraged him to take the children to a doctor in the morning. I left him with the verse, Joshua 1:9, "Be strong and courageous. Do not be afraid; do not be discouraged. For the Lord your God will be with you wherever you go."

"How are the children doing? Did they see a doctor?" I asked the next morning.

"Yes, Mom, they did and had their blood checked. The doctor found they had typhoid and malaria in their system and gave them a treatment. I'll send receipts," he replied. Malaria and typhoid were common, and I was thankful there were medical treatments available.

I then asked, "And how are you feeling?"

His response encouraged me. "Just like the words of Joshua, the Lord is with me, and I am now feeling better. My Sunday was so wonderful . . . full of God's grace! The worship was wonderful!"

It made me glad to hear of the joy he experienced in worship. Yet the news of the world had its effect even on Kakembo.

"I don't usually read news, but I was shocked to read about what is happening in Ukraine, Mom! I am praying for them, and it hurts me so much to hear about the children and orphans suffering," Kakembo messaged.

I had recently read about stories of men who waited in vans at Ukrainian borders, posing as pastors, with the intent of child sex trafficking. This was horrendous news! It made me appreciate the nurture and loving care our thirty-three orphans were receiving all the more. I was so grateful to God for allowing us to help shield these precious children from the evils of the world!

"I understand how you must feel. It's a good time to memorize Psalm 91," I reminded him. I had personalized and memorized that chapter three years ago, and I found it a real comfort to me as I pondered the scary world news about a potential World War III. I had been repeating the verses, reminding myself:

> I shall not be afraid of the terror at night nor of the arrow that flies by day. A thousand may fall at my right hand, and ten thousand at my left, but it shall not approach me. I will only look on and see the recompense of the wicked!

Recalling these verses and personalizing them put my mind at peace in this volatile and uncertain world with constant talk of war in the media.

"My day has been quite tiresome, Mom! I had to do research on making windows and doors. I went from one place to another to finally find a good price! I found a man who is a Christian, and he is very good at making them and at a good price. He was so happy to meet me, and he advised me so much about the making of windows," Kakembo reported.

Not only was he learning a lot about managing a building project, but Kakembo was also gaining knowledge about the trades that go with it. It did my heart good to know that we would be providing business to a Christian man in the construction trade of doors and windows in Mityana. Businesses were still suffering badly from the outbreak of COVID-19. No doubt, it pleased Kakembo as well to provide work for a Christian brother.

"You are becoming well-known in your community!" I quipped. "Yes, indeed I am. Indeed I am, Mom!" was his reply. "I was so exhausted yesterday that I came home and went straight to bed!"

"You are needing extra sleep," I assured him. I knew he was putting many miles on his bike, and that night I discovered he didn't get back until 8:30 p.m. in the pouring rain! So it didn't surprise me one bit when he stopped his message to me mid-sentence. He was no doubt doing that "Kakembo thing," falling asleep in the very middle of his text!

Kakembo had been working so incredibly hard, and yet he remained very grateful and delighted to see the future children's home materializing before his very eyes. It was a wonderful miracle of God to him and me! The next morning I was surprised to hear from him at such an early time.

"I am already at the site early this morning waiting for the trucks that are bringing cement and stones. Today I am going to be super busy buying materials for making the floors," he went on.

"And will you put some sort of tile on top of the cement floor?" I asked.

"Absolutely! Have I used that vocabulary well?" he asked.

"Absolutely!" I answered, chuckling to myself. However, as funds were becoming tight, I reminded myself this was the Lord's project, not mine, and He would provide. Indeed He did provide for tiles, ceramic tiles, much more beautiful and an easier way to keep floors clean for the children's sake! It ended up that ceramic tiles were sold wholesale in the nearby city of Kampala at a slightly higher price as cheaply made ones in Mityana!

That evening I received a photo and wasn't sure what I was looking at. It appeared to be pieces of a snake. "Is that a snake?" I squealed inwardly.

Kakembo acknowledged, "Yes, Mom; the builders killed two snakes as they were coming from the bushes in the bordering forest. They advised me to put a fence up to avoid snakes biting the children."

"Yikes!" I reacted. One snake would be bad enough, but two? Bob did a web search on snakes in Uganda and discovered there were numerous venomous ones, including the green and black mamba and the Gaboon viper.

Kakembo had already warned me about the local monkeys who steal bananas, but it concerned me more when I read about wild cats and the great forest hog potentially living in the forest area!

Forest hogs were very closely related to the javelinas found in the state of Arizona, and they can be aggressive. However, Ugandan forest hogs are larger and have tusks protruding from the mouth.

Theft was also a concern. Kakembo had experienced that already with thieves stealing several of the chickens they had raised. We decided a brick wall around the house was assuredly a wise investment to protect the children!

I was grateful brick was still rather inexpensive as it turned out to be quite the walled fence! The bricks were made close by in a brick-made oven using the red clay soil. It would need a cover of cement to keep it from eroding. It left me with a secure feeling knowing the children would be out of harm's way!

PASTOR'S HEALTH & DAILY LIFE

"**HOW WAS YOUR** Sunday?" I asked Kakembo. "My Sunday has been wonderful! We had a good service, and I preached on Galatians 5 about the fruit of the Spirit," he answered. "I spoke about verse 16, where He wants us to walk in the Spirit and not in the flesh. The flesh conflicts with the Spirit and only leads to spiritual death. I see many people in my community choosing the path of desiring material things but not spiritual things."

No doubt, I thought, even Christians in poor countries have that spiritual battle to contend with. How so much more in the rich countries!

"I just received a message from Mrs. Ssemwogelere that Pastor is not well," I continued to read. "He is having so much pain in the stomach and is losing weight and is weak due to vomiting and diarrhea."

"Oh no, is he able to go to the hospital?" I asked.

"I am worried about my godfather," Kakembo replied. "His wife and daughter are caring for him. But I am renting a taxi to take him to the hospital and help with medicine as they don't have enough money."

I was thankful Kakembo could help through our funding, but I was concerned for the money's sake as funds were getting low. I knew, however, that Pastor Ssemwogelere meant the world to Kakembo. As it turned out, it was critical for the pastor to be treated for typhoid and high blood pressure.

Kakembo shared with me earlier that the pastor's blood pressure had given him a lot of problems ever since the eviction incident. The hospitalization turned out to be crucial, and Kakembo's compassion for his godfather was clearly evident!

No doubt, he had a lot of love and respect for this dear man who had given so much of his life to the orphanage. Thankfully, the pastor was able to return home after three nights.

I learned later that he was very thrilled about the orphanage building project, and I was looking so very forward to meet this dear godly man and his wife and to hear their life story in a future visit, Lord willing!

"I love seeing the photo of you and Joseph together!" I commented after viewing the snapshot Kakembo sent. "Your beard is getting a little longer," I teased.

"Hahaha, yes, Mom. The beard is growing so fast, especially these days when I spend so much time at the site!" he acknowledged. I would wholeheartedly agree with his statement about his time! I was viewing many photos of brick, mortar, and expense receipts that he sent nightly. It was genuinely good to see a photo of these two energetic and caring brothers together!

I was getting anxious to have the building completed so I could see the beautiful faces of the children again. My desire to visit them was growing stronger and stronger. I really did long to see the children and hug each and every one of them!

Instead, I was looking at bricks, metal, plumbing pipes, receipts, and so on, things geared to the male side of things and important to Kakembo, Joseph, and Bob. It was amazing to see their beautiful home materializing before my very eyes!

Joseph walked the children a long distance to school early mornings and then back again, arriving in the early evening. Kakembo needed to be at the building site to keep the workers on their toes as well as making sure supplies were on hand. The speed of their work lagged when he wasn't around, and time was of the essence! He kept the workers on their toes!

When Kakembo's day ended, the kids were asleep for the night, leaving no time for photos. It was also becoming more frequent for him to fall asleep mid-sentence while texting during our nighttime conversations! He would apologize the following day, and I would tease him, saying, "It's that 'Kakembo thing' again!" followed with a crazy face icon.

This young man was working so very hard and so diligently that it didn't take but a few seconds for him to fall asleep once his head hit the pillow! How I wish I could do that myself! Even my husband, Bob, had the same ability.

"How can you fall asleep so quickly?" I would ask exasperated at times when it frequently took me an hour or two. Bob's answer was always, "It's cuz I have a clear conscience!" Ha! Perhaps it was the same for dear Kakembo.

A Refuge

"**Hello, Mom, how** was your day?" His usual words greeted me.

"I had a good day. How is Joseph and Brenda?" I replied.

"Brenda is okay, but she was telling me that her friend from church was facing serious problems. Her father died several months ago, and now her uncle has chased her away from her father's house. She is being mistreated and beaten and denied the chance to continue her education, and she is now living on the streets," Kakembo continued.

"Oh no! How sad! How can you help?" I empathized.

"I was thinking of telling her to come to the orphanage, Mom, for refuge," he answered.

"It would be good if she could stay and help Brenda with the children. But careful, son . . . I've been praying that the Lord would bring a wife your way!" I teased.

Oh . . . dear Mom! I don't even know her! All I know is she loves Jesus and is a born-again Christian who has attended our church . . . and she needs help!" he quipped.

"Hmm? Born-again Christian, eh?" I teased.

"You're kidding, right?" he asked with the crazy faces following.

"Yes," I assured him. "But I confess I have been praying the Lord will lead the right one your way at the right time," I confided.

In my heart, I knew it would have to be a **very** special woman who would love the children and the Lord as much as he did; indeed, a rare young woman to find.

The next day, I inquired if the woman had taken refuge at the orphanage. "Sadly, she hasn't been found yet," was his reply. Her name was Nagawa. Bob and I kept this dear young woman in our evening prayers.

Since it was the weekend, I reminded Kakembo that maybe he could take a break from sermon preparation and take photos of the children for me. The next morning, he didn't disappoint, and I was delighted to see the beautiful faces of two of the children we had provided medical care. "You know how to make this mountain mama happy!" I beamed.

"It brings me joy to make you happy," was his sweet reply. And I was truly so thrilled to see their darling photos! And so was Bob! It was a wonderful reminder as to why we were putting so much effort into a building. The children were worth all that effort and expense!

It brought such cheer to see their faces. I truly love the pure essence of gladness that the Lord was giving me. There is no comparison to the world's counterfeit attempts for joy!

"Praying the children won't have to walk that long distance to school in the rain today," I messaged.

"Well the children haven't gone to school today cause we are experiencing heavy rainfall," was his reply.

"Oh dear, I'm sure they aren't unhappy about that!" I joked.

"Yes, Mom," Kakembo responded. "They are so happy and have run back to their beds shouting and laughing!" I was sure they were indeed laughing, with glee, no doubt!

I learned that the next day was very rainy as well, as his comments stated, "The kids are missing school again as we can't afford them getting sick while walking long distances in the cold rain."

My heart yearned for more resources to provide a van and prayed that a kind Christian person with means in the community would see the children walking so far and provide for this need. But there weren't many there who had the means, unfortunately. Kakembo, nevertheless, kept to his building schedule, riding his bike to the site daily, even in the downpours!

"We are praying the Lord's blessings and protection over you," I texted. "Dress warm and please take care on your bike!" I stressed.

"Yes, the clay roads do get slippery here!" he replied. "Yesterday I was going so fast on my bike that I almost hit a wild rabbit!"

"Hmm. Pity! You could have had rabbit stew!" I joked.

"Hahahaha...indeed! I would have taken it to the building workers to cook," he laughed.

"Oh yes! Rabbit stew with black tire seasoning!" I added. I chuckled at the comical and crazy face icons he sent.

"Wasuze otya, Mama? [Did you sleep well, Mom?]" I just feel like asking you how can I pray for you, for all you have done for me? I just wish I was rich to give on my wealth," read Kakembo's message. I was moved that he wanted so much to give something that he considered of great worth.

I told him to pray that "my life would be rich by bringing the Lord glory . . . just as you do, dear!" His reply stunned me!

"It already is . . . you and Dad are bringing glory to Him, and you're bringing much light into so many people's lives here, more than you can imagine. Please continue being the light in our lives! You don't know how many people I have led to Christ due to the work you're doing in our lives, Mom."

I cried! I never realized the spiritual fruit-bearing I would have missed if I had previously chosen to ignore Kakembo's first messages! The Lord was teaching me that Bob and I were just one part of a bigger plan. This young man was the instrument God was using with his feet to the ground in working so hard to care for his precious children and to bring souls to Christ.

I told Kakembo we would be doing lots of hugging in heaven, and I assured him his mansion would be far grander than mine! His crown would contain far more precious jewels! And there would be lots of singing and dancing! Bob and I would be embracing every one of the beautiful children, along with Brenda, Joseph, and dear Kakembo, not to mention every soul they led to Christ! It would be a grand crowd! And we'd dance, jive, and jump while singing loud hallelujahs to Jesus our Lord and Savior! What a glorious future we would have!

> Sing to God, sing in praise of His name, extol Him who rides on the clouds; Rejoice before Him—His name is the Lord. A Father to the fatherless, a defender of widows, is God in His holy dwelling. God sets the lonely in families" (Ps. 68:4–6).

I had been wondering about the young woman, Nagawa, who had fled from her abusive uncle. We were praying for her protection as she tried to live on the streets. So it was a relief when I received Kakembo's message, "Yesterday Brenda's friend, Nagawa, came to the orphanage. She was found . . ."

I replied that I was so happy she was found. Kakembo responded, "Oh, thank you for praying for her. The streets may have been so cold and dangerous. But she feels safe now." Yet I knew that perhaps another mouth to feed may have been a concern for this caring young man. Nevertheless, his heart always reached out to the unfortunate!

"Hopefully, she can be of help at the orphanage," I mentioned.

"I hope so, Mom," Kakembo replied. She is God-fearing and a born-again Christian."

I often wondered how dear Brenda managed with cooking, cleaning, and laundry by hand for thirty-three children and three adults! Truly she was an incredible woman of God! I knew, though, that Brenda and Joseph were valuable help as well in the care of these children.

Bob and I made it a habit to pray for these caregivers and the children morning and night. We continued to cover them in the protection and blessing of the Lord Jesus Christ. At times, I wondered, "Are our prayers making a difference, Lord?"

It was with such gratitude I received the message from Kakembo, saying, "Hello, Mom. You don't know the happiness you bring to our hearts. We were always rejected before, but God is doing miracles! When I look at the house, I can't believe it is ours! The kids have been having good health, and they no longer are falling sick as easily as before. I strongly believe your prayers are the answer to my cries when I was in the hospital while crying out to God with a bleeding heart."

I thanked God for that affirmation that our prayers were, in fact, being heard and that His grace and favor were being given to the orphanage and caregivers!

Later, as I wished him a blessed day with God's favor, he commented, "I know it will be a blessed day with favor as I know the Lord is answering your prayers."

His faith ignited the spark to my faith to continue in prayer for the continuation of all God was doing for them!

Later, Kakembo sent me a photo, saying, "This photo reminded me of where Joseph and I were at one time." The photo said it all!

"Has Nagawa had any more trouble from her uncle?" I asked.

"No, Mom. Nagawa is doing better nowadays. We heard news that he has sold everything that was left behind by her father."

"So she won't be receiving anything from her father's estate? How about the house? I would think that should belong to her legally," I lamented.

"We were hoping she would receive something, but here in Africa, a girl child suffers a lot when her father dies. They also face a lot of violence," he replied.

It saddened me to read his comments. I later read that in Uganda, women seldom own land or houses due to devastatingly unequal inheritance laws and gender inequality. Many times relatives take advantage of these women's vulnerable situations through sexual abuse.

Answering my question as to how things were going, Kakembo answered, "We thank the Almighty Lord that He has been keeping us happy and blessed. The kids have started with the school term exams."

I assured him we were praying continually for the children to remember their studies for the exams. I asked, "Are things going better for Nagawa?"

"Yes, dear Mom, and now that she is being surrounded by people here who care and love her, she is doing ok. She is of good help at the orphanage, and she has been so hard-working lately. She loves taking and bringing the children from school! She also walks to the worksite to cook lunch for the workers."

Hmm, a young hard-working woman who loves the Lord and loves the children? My mind contemplated the possibilities, but I kept my thoughts to myself.

The last thing my mutabani (son) in Christ needed during his incredibly busy time was for this mountain mama to create matchmaking duress on his already stressed and busy schedule! Nevertheless, I couldn't help wonder...perhaps . . .?

Travel, Trials, & Interruptions

KAKEMBO WAS GOING every single day to the work site to keep builders working at the speed he wanted. It was mid-March, and he had not had a day off since the beginning of construction in January!

I was worried about him overdoing it and prayed the Lord would sustain him physically, mentally, and spiritually. Thankfully, Joseph was able to pitch in where needed, and I was so pleased to hear he had taken on preaching on Sundays, freeing Kakembo's time.

As construction progressed, I was amazed at how much cement and sand were used! Photos showed huge dump loads of sand on the grounds.

Due to the brittleness of the baked bricks, a cement plaster needed to be added to the inside and outside walls of the house, followed up with moisture resistant paint. I imagined, with paint and flooring, the house could truly look like a home! However, with each passing day, prices continued to climb, and cement was now beginning to be rationed due to the short supply.

We were thankful the Lord timed it so most of the building bricks and cement were in place before the high rise in prices.

As the building was nearing completion, talk between Bob and me about visiting the orphanage became more frequent. We were discouraged, however, about the length of time it would involve in an airplane, about twenty-four hours from New York!

These older bodies trying to conform to a very small space in a very confined environment for that many hours would no doubt feel the lingering effects for days. We'd probably get the body kinks out just in time for our return trip home! I was nearing age sixty-nine and Bob seventy-three, so we knew if we were going to plan the trip, it had to be sooner, and not later! Time was not necessarily our friend in that regard.

Having lived in Italy, we knew in advance that cultural differences would also be markedly felt. I remember when I first arrived in Italy how I craved ice for my drinks. Anything ordered in terms of cold drinks at cafes were basically lukewarm. Many Italians thought it odd to add ice to drinks. During those warm days, I literally went through withdrawal symptoms for a good ice-cold drink!

Other common conveniences in the US, like air conditioning, would be in short supply in Uganda as it was in Italy. It would be warm and humid in equatorial Africa, and the shores of Lake Victoria would be close by. The clammy moist climate would be something my body wasn't used to, but we could certainly handle one week!

The desire to see and hug the children, to see Kakembo and give a real-life flesh-and-blood hug to this dear son in Christ, along with Brenda, Joseph, and Nagawa kept growing inside me! Bob and I would love to meet Pastor Ssemwogelere and his wife and hear their life stories! I was also anxious to see the new orphanage home that we and Kakembo worked so hard in bringing to fruition!

A trip there would bring such a sense of happiness and fulfillment for us. So despite the obstacles, it didn't take long before Bob and I were both persuaded that a trip would be a very important chapter to this God-journey. We began to make arrangements even before the construction of the orphanage was complete. I didn't want to let Kakembo know yet as he was already so burdened with all the details of finishing the work!

I began buying children's clothing, as well as jump ropes, inflatable balls, sunglasses, children's books, CDs, and craft items. I added hot chocolate mixes, spices, over-the-counter medicines, tooth brushes and toothpaste, lotions, and every other thing I thought might be beneficial, along with special gifts for the four adults.

It didn't take long to find I had completely filled two large suitcases with what I deemed was beneficial. So much for leaving room for my stuff!

We went to the Health District and got our vaccines like champions! Our bodies were anti-bodied to the hilt! Typhoid, malaria, and hepatitis didn't stand a chance now! Not to mention COVID-19!

The daily news was certainly beginning to take a toll on our emotions in the coming weeks. Costs were increasing everywhere due to the war in Ukraine, and stocks were crashing, not a great combination to feed my faith! So I was dismayed at reading Kakembo's response when I asked him, "How are things going your way?"

"Stressed, my dear!" Kakembo responded. Brenda called saying Baby Tricia had a high temperature. I had to rush back to the orphanage to take her to the hospital."

I was troubled to hear of the news! We had gone for quite some time without illness, and now little Tricia had come down with malaria and had a very high fever. She had also been losing weight. I didn't recognize her photo since she looked so much smaller. But with Kakembo getting her proper medication and treatments, she would recover.

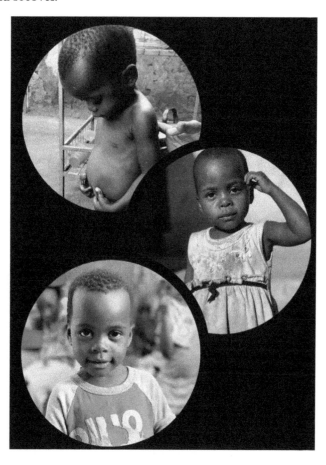

I loved the previous photos of baby Tricia's healthier days. It was not hard to love this cherub-looking face and dreamy eyes! What a sweetheart! I'd love to hold her in my arms!

I also received a recent photo of Kasumba. I remembered the days about eight months earlier when this dear boy was dying in the hospital from malaria.

You may remember my story in the beginning of this book. The orphanage had no funds to pay for the medicine and treatments at that time, and the Lord used us to intervene for this very critical need. It did my heart so good to see Kasumba, or Joseph Kasumba, now as a healthy and good-looking boy! Bob and I both pray and believe that the Lord will have a good future for this attractive boy.

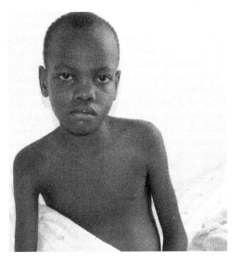 

Along with being stressed about baby Tricia's health, Kakembo shared that a thief had broken into the new building by cutting off a padlock and had stolen ten boxes of floor tiles! It was an exasperating ordeal that interrupted the progress of the work, not to mention the loss of a significant amount of money.

Kakembo had gone to great lengths to shop for floor tiles that would be reasonably priced at a wholesale dealer. This required him to go to the large city of Kampala by bus, which was always a long and chaotic trip.

He shared that after they went to the police to report the theft, the police required he pay a fee so they could then get a dog to track down the crook. It would all be in vain, however, as Kakembo reported, "They are so corrupt, Mom. When they find the thief, they'll just get more bribe money from him and let him go anyway!"

So much for justice! My daily reading in a Ugandan news website, only confirms the corruption that infiltrates the police and politicians. Bribes rule!

The tiles would have to be replaced. My prayer was for peace in all the disruption that was caused by this thief, and I placed the situation in the Lord's hands.

Nagawa continued walking to the building site to cook a meal for the workers as she was able. Some days, the downpour of rain hindered her. It was a long walk, and cooking was rudimentary, over a fire. I was beginning to see how hard this young woman was working and how willing she was to help in whatever way she could.

Nagawa would also walk the children to school when necessary, and they were beginning to love her as a sister. She proved to be invaluable, and especially during a time when Brenda had to have to leave the orphanage. She was needed to help care for Mrs. Ssemwogelere, the pastor's wife, who had been bitten by a poisonous snake, causing her leg to become severely swollen. Nagawa took Brenda's place in caring for the children and cooking the orphanage meals. In time, I saw how much Kakembo valued her as a hard-working sister in Christ.

I woke up to read Kakembo's greeting, "Hello dear Mom. How are you? It's been raining cats and dogs here!"

I got a kick out of his use of English idioms and responded, "It's been raining cats and dogs here too, and maybe even some chickens and pigs!" He laughed and commented on the coincidence of it raining hard in Idaho and Uganda at the same time.

During the torrential rains, it was discovered that one side wall of the house was retaining too much moisture. The builder advised a rock support to the base of the wall that would help keep the rain from soaking into the wall. It ended up being a very attractive addition with a ledge around the house for the children to sit and eat outdoors.

However, it was one more delay in the finishing of the house. I was beginning to wonder if our planned trip to Uganda during the first week in June would be too soon. We only had three weeks to go.

It was Mother's Day, and I had a very good and special time with my mother as well as my daughter, Monica. I wondered if they celebrated Mother's Day in Uganda.

I looked at my phone later and noticed I had missed several video calls from Kakembo! To my dismay, I realized too late that my volume was lowered, and I hadn't been alerted by the sound.

I was so disappointed about missing the calls. Nevertheless, I was thrilled with the many photos he sent!

Indeed they did celebrate Mother's Day, and they had a special cake made in my honor. The kids had even made me cards, which I so enjoyed reading by photos.

I was so surprised and deeply touched. It was times like these that my heart was overwhelmed with affection for these beautiful children and young adults and for the love they showed me.

They kids were all dressed up for the occasion. The photos were precious!

I was pleased, as well, to see Kakembo was able to spend some time with the children. He had been so engaged with the work that he had very little time to enjoy their company.

The following days were consumed with the electrical and plumbing provisions. It would be a luxury for them to have electrical lighting in the rooms. And after floor tiles were completed the indoor, painting would begin.

The difference in the beauty of the new rooms was a stark contrast from what their current rooms looked like! The present unfinished cement walls and floors were dimly lit with the kerosene lanterns they had to use. Whereas the rooms in the new house would be brightly painted with ceiling lights!

The Lord had brought a new Christian young man, Ronald, into their lives. Ronald, who was an interior designer, felt the Lord was telling him in a dream to give to the poor! After meeting Joseph and learning about the orphanage, he wanted to donate his time and talent to paint the interior walls. I was amazed at the goodness of the Lord in adding his beautiful touches to the house! What a wonderful gift!

Time was getting very short before the required move-out of the current building. It became apparent to me that our planned visit may only add more stress to an already stressful situation. So I was very pleasantly surprised when Kakembo sent his message that "the Court sent someone to survey the situation and told us we can stay until the end of June." Praise God, that added another month to get things completed!

I then revealed to Kakembo that we were making arrangements to come and visit the first of June and that I had taken care of everything so as not to burden him as we found a furnished house on the outskirts of Mityana online through Airbnb.

Kakembo replied, "I think it would be better for me to see the place before you come, Mom. Some places here are not safe, and we need to take a serious look at everything. I want to make sure the beds do not have bedbugs." I so appreciated his concern for our safety.

After viewing the place, Kakembo informed me that although the house looked nice, it was much too long a distance from the orphanage. He and Joseph had to rent a boda boda driver for transportation there. I could envision the three of them piled on the small motorcycle.

He went on to say, "That area scares me too as it's near an area village where they have night dancers, and there is no security fence around the house."

I asked him, "What in the world are night dancers?" I was shocked with his explanation. "They are people with demons who walk naked at night, doing all kinds of evil things!"

My search on the internet revealed that there were indeed "night dancers" in certain village areas of Uganda! It served to remind me that spiritual darkness is found in every culture in various forms, some stranger than others. In fact, the events in the US are getting more bizarrely evil each and every day!

MONITOR

Reviews & Profiles

Bukunja: The infamous land of 'night dancers'

Thursday, July 03, 2014 — updated on January 05, 2021

As the world gets spiritually darker, whether in poor or rich nations, evil persists. What a comfort to know we can be shielded by the presence of the Most High!

Psalm 91 tells us that we can rest under the shadow of His wings as we dwell in companionship with Him. He will command His guardian angels to watch our steps along the way. We need not fear, even though war breaks out around us.

I learned that Joseph would be gone the first two weeks of June as he would be joining Pastor Ssemwogelere for an evangelistic crusade in the Fort Portal area located in the western region. It pleased me to hear Joseph was going with the pastor getting some firsthand training and evangelistic experience. We certainly did not want to miss out on seeing Joseph and meeting the pastor on our visit! So we determined a July trip would be better.

"I suggest, Mom, that we finish the new orphanage home first. Then we can prepare a room for you and Dad. The kids will be having a school break in late July, so the kids and everyone could spend more time with you both at that time," Kakembo replied.

It seemed July would be a much better-suited time to visit, but I had my doubts about there being room for two additional bodies added to the current thirty-seven residents!

Kakembo's message the morning of June 3 really concerned me. He informed me that he received an emergency call from the school. One of his boys, Josaya, was showing signs of severe illness.

Besides vomiting, he was unable to stand, and kept falling to the ground hitting his head several times! Since Brenda was still away, Kakembo called a woman who attended their church to help Nagawa with Josaya.

His videos showed poor little Josaya on the ground without clothing, crying deliriously and tossing frantically while the woman friend was trying to dress him for the hospital.

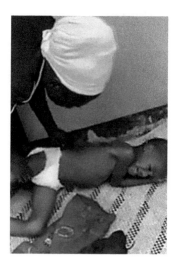

Later, I received Kakembo's note. "I slept in the hospital with him, so he can access treatments at night. I have been up and down all night to give him drinks to stay hydrated, but he is vomiting so much! Joseph will be returning from the evangelistic crusade, and Brenda will also be returning to help out." I breathed a sigh of relief to hear Brenda and Joseph were returning to assist him.

Kakembo had such a tender love for the kids. And he would once again be at the side of one of his dear little ones suffering through difficult nights in the hospital.

He later confirmed "Josaya has bad malaria. It seemed at times the illness just went to his head! I was afraid and thought he was going mad!"

His comment confused me at first, but then I realized just how uncontrollable little Josaya had been, no doubt in part due to a very high fever. I was alarmed in my internet searches about the high number of children under the age of five who die in Africa each year from the effects of malaria.

Nevertheless, Kakembo reassured me that the Lord would get him through this as He had done in previous times. "Sometimes I feel so down and so weak whenever I see the children like this! But I stay strong with the Lord's help. I have to be strong for them!"

After we shared Scriptures together, he ended by saying, "I will read His Word for Josaya and me before going to sleep." The Word of God was a comfort to him, and he always turned to his Bible in formidable times. Truly it is in the toughest times that the Lord does His deepest work in us.

After some "touch and go," Joseph was able to relieve Kakembo at the hospital to let him resume working at the site. After over a week, I was so relieved to hear Josaya was feeling much better.

I replied, "Neeyanzizza nnyo (I am so grateful) for the good news that Josaya is doing much better!" I had been doing some online learning of Luganda phrases, and it was fun to add them to our chit chats.

Kakembo reported that the crusade was going very well for Pastor Ssemwogelere and that many were coming to know Christ personally! I later learned that after several nights of many people attending but not responding to the salvation messages, that the pastor woke Joseph in the middle of the night, telling him that the two of them needed to pray that night against the resistant spiritual ambiance.

Joseph shared that eventually hundreds of decisions to follow Christ were made! Needless to say, it left an indelible impression as to how important prayer is in spiritual matters like these!

I regretted that Joseph was not able to attend the conclusion of the crusade. Yet I felt very grateful that he was allowed to see God's work there and still return in time to assist with duties at the orphanage. What a team . . . holding each other up during difficult times! And praise God the crusade bore much fruit!

A June Surprise!

JUNE WAS A very busy month trying to tie ends up in the finishing of the house. On the last Sunday in June, I heard from Kakembo with this text, "Good morning, Mom. I have a surprise for you before you go to church!" He then called me using video chat via Messenger.

What a surprise and delight to see all the children sitting on the floor in their new sitting room! Then music came on, and the children rose and began dancing! Of course, Joseph and Kakembo were dancing as well with so much joy!

It was so fun to interact with them during the video chat! Delightful photos followed, showing Brenda and Nagawa preparing the rice while the children enjoyed their evening special meal at their new home.

I had no idea they had done the big move! What gratification to see the fruit of our giving, all the prayers, and their hard, hard labor!

The move was done just in the nick of time and was no doubt harried at best. We learned later that the new owners refused to allow the water tank to be moved. In essence, they were stealing it, along with other items that had to be left behind!

The walk to school had increased to about an hour, so it wasn't surprising to hear that the smaller children were frequently crying and having to be carried. A good stretch of the walk was on a busy dusty road with passing trucks, boda bodas, and people shopping in the stalls on the side of the road. Intermixed with this were tied-up goats and chickens being sold in small cages, along with roaming stray dogs. It was dangerous, and the adults and older children had to keep a very watchful eye on the kids in the busy chaos of this daily walk.

The kids' school clothes had to be washed daily due to all the dust, not to mention the coughing and runny noses. It only impressed me more about their critical need for some kind of van for transportation.

Father, Guide, Advisor, & Shepherd

KAKEMBO HADN'T BEEN aware of the emotional turmoil the pastor was going through in the months leading up to the crusade. He was beginning to have some serious episodes of high blood pressure. It was during a time in the hospital that the pastor surprised Kakembo by asking for forgiveness for a big mistake he had made.

In an effort to bring in more crops to sell for income, the pastor used the small humble church building with land as collateral to take out a loan to rent more crop land and invest in seed and fertilizers. Little did he know that the normal rains would be replaced with a very dry and hot growing season. Many farmers' crops failed, and he, too, did not succeed in his planting venture.

Since he was unable to pay the loan back, the loaner took possession of the church plot. I had been reading as well about the scrupulous lenders who charge exorbitant interest.

It broke the pastor's heart that he was unable to leave the small church parcel to Kakembo and Joseph.

At that time, about twenty-five adults, in addition to children, were attending the humble hut-like building. Kakembo and Joseph were leading services and preaching.

All of this stress, in addition to the prior eviction from the former orphanage residence, weighed very heavily on the pastor's heart. Soon he began to experience dangerous levels of high blood pressure.

I somberly read Kakembo's text on July 19. "Hello, Mom, how are you doing? Am having a bad day, and we have slept in the hospital. Pastor Ssemwogelere's condition is really bad, and we really need your prayers, Mom!

"I was called this evening. His condition has worsened. I rushed there and found the pastor in a critical condition. We are in the hospital now praying for him to gain his consciousness."

"Oh son, we will be praying hard! We hold on to Isaiah 41:10. 'So do not fear, for I am with you. Do not be dismayed, for I am your God. I will strengthen you and help you. I will uphold you with My righteous right hand.' Trying to bring some hope, I reminded him of God's promises. But hope was slim.

After a very difficult day and night at the hospital, Kakembo eventually needed to return to the orphanage to clean up and eat. They would take turns doing this.

The next morning on my end, I was stunned to see that he had tried calling me numerous times via Facebook Messenger! I had inadvertently turned the sound off my cell phone.

Later, I received a phone call from my dear Alaskan friend, Susan, who had previously given towards the orphanage needs. She and Kakembo had then became acquainted through Messenger, and she was such a prayer supporter and encourager to Kakembo.

She said Kakembo had reached her late at night and was in great distress. He told her he was frantically trying to reach me as he wanted to tell me that the pastor had died during the night.

Kakembo wasn't at the hospital at the pastor's death as he had left to clean up and rest a bit. Joseph, Brenda, Mrs. Ssemwogelere, and Nagawa were there. It really tore Kakembo up emotionally when he heard that the pastor had called out for him and that he then slipped away into the hands of the Lord during Kakembo's absence!

I immediately called him to tell him that I was so sorry that I wasn't there for him! He was able to say only a few words to me, and then began sobbing, having to end the call as he was unable to talk.

His following texts read, "But I don't know why the Lord let this to happen to me? Pastor wanted to talk to me in his last moments, and I wasn't there! We have lost our father, our guide, our advisor, our shepherd, our everything! He is the reason why we are here today. I can't stand the pain, Mom! He has left us, but why!?"

I was at a loss for words but assured him that it was very likely that the pastor wanted to tell him how proud he was of the young godly man he had become and to thank him for his dedicated care he gave to the children.

I remembered something I heard a pastor once say, "'Though I walk through the valley of the shadow of death, I fear no evil for You are with me' (Ps. 23:4 NASB), and what I found was that there are measures of His presence that you can **only** find in the valley of the shadow of death." I shared these thoughts with him.

"Son, I'm praying His presence will be with all of you and that you and the family will sense His loving arms around you even during your grief. Know that He knows and feels your deep sorrow. He experienced it Himself. The Lord knows our weaknesses."

I reminded him the Lord was placing every one of his tears in His bottle. "Let your tears flow freely, son. The Lord has you in His loving arms even though you may be feeling betrayal by Him. This is natural to feel that way."

They were only words that I was sure could not penetrate or relieve his pain and heartache at that moment. His beloved and godly father figure was gone.

Nevertheless, I knew the Lord was, in fact, in their presence, watching with full compassion and understanding, knowing well the profound sadness they were going through.

At Lazarus's death, Jesus, knowing deep sorrow, wept too. Imagine: the Lord God, the coming King and Lord over the power of death, was crying at the death of his beloved friend!

Kakembo sent a photo of the pastor, saying, "This was the last time I saw him smiling. We will be paying the hospital bills and taking him to the mortuary. Pastor will be buried in his ancestral home in a village near Jinja." I was so sad I wouldn't be able to sit down with this godly man and hear his life story.

"We will be starting the day-long journey tomorrow," he went on. "The school director has given the kids time off to finish the burial and allowed us to use a relative's van to take his body there. We have a friend with a car as well, and we are all going, including the children."

Two days later, I read, "We have reached Pastor Ssemwogelere's father's home. Family and friends have been coming through to say goodbye and to see him for the last time. Tomorrow we will be laying his body in the ground."

I learned Pastor's father's home was a humble one. The father had passed years earlier and had a son and family living in the old home, trying to grow crops during this warm season. Water was very scarce, and they had to haul it from a distant stream.

Kakembo shared that people were sleeping on the ground and the floors of the house. The children were frightened by the whole ordeal, especially seeing the pastor's body lying in a wooden coffin to be viewed by all. People gathered to show love and say their last goodbyes. Pastor Ssemwogelere was loved and respected by many.

"Today we have laid him to rest forever, Mom. We are only left with memories and photos," Kakembo reported. It was July 25, 2022.

"I wish it was a happier day for you. Happy birthday, son," I mentioned. He had just turned twenty-six. "Oh I had forgotten! I had no time to remember. Thank you, Mom, and may the Lord bless you for remembering," he replied.

It was obvious we had to reschedule our trip. I tried to buy airline tickets once again for the first part of August and was utterly shocked to see how much prices had increased. The price of one ticket had increased about as much as the previous price of two!

Savings were low at this point, so Bob and I had a serious discussion. With great reluctance on Bob's part, we finally agreed that I would go by myself after assuring Bob of reservations at safe hotels and good shuttle services shown online. Kakembo ensured me he would be picking me up in a rented van to take me to Mityana.

It would be a brutally long flight from Seattle to Qatar, a long layover, and then to Entebbe with a total of twenty-eight hours! The return trip was even longer. I was a little week in the knees at the thought, but my heart was beating strong, saying, "Go for it!"

I let Kakembo know I had delayed our trip again and had decided that it would be best that due to increased costs that only I come. Kakembo countered, "Oh no, dear Mom! Won't it be a lonely trip for you? Please try to come with Dad when you come. We really want to see you both. I'm afraid for you to travel alone! I'm so sorry for the changes as I know they have cost so much more for you!" Kakembo moaned.

I became more concerned for him. This change of plans added additional worries to his already over-burdened and emotionally fragile heart.

Kakembo carried a great deal of stress and sorrow. Due to that, he frequently had a lot of pain in his stomach, which may have been due to ulcers. His stomach was giving him problems during the funeral trip. I had previously introduced him to buying antacids from a pharmacy and was happy to hear that had given him past relief. However, there was no pharmacy or doctor close by in that village.

"The family has given me local herbs to take here, but they are so sour," Kakembo said. It sounded to me like something I certainly wouldn't want to take with an ulcer! But I suppose using herbs goes with the territory due to traditional practices and the lack of medicine in Uganda Even I believe in medicinal herbs but usually in capsule form! At any rate, I suggested he drink some milk, and that seemed to do the trick for the moment. Be that as it may, stress was a trigger point to his stomachaches. And continual stress was what he seemed to be experiencing for months on end!

It was decided that Brenda, along with the older children, would stay with Mrs. Ssemwogelere at the ancestral home where the pastor's brother and family were living. It was a very simple farm where the pastor's wife could stay for a while.

Brenda and the kids would be a great comfort for this grieving widow. They would also help in planting their crops and hauling water from the outlying almost-dry stream.

The rainy season would hopefully come soon, and they were certainly praying for the much-needed moisture! I was so sad I would miss seeing Brenda and the older kids, but I knew she was an essential help.

Uganda or Bust!

"Hello, son," I texted. "I just landed in Doha, Qatar,

after a twelve-hour flight. Other than the crying child behind me, the trip went well, and I was actually able to sleep some. I have an eight-hour layover, then a six-hour flight to Entebbe. Qatar is a crazy rich city!

This airport is amazing! I feel somewhat like a pauper here!" I added. I sent photos of the gold shops and other glitzy stores in the amazing, shiny, and spotless terminal.

"Hahaha. I know how you feel!" he replied. No doubt he did! I would soon learn there would not be even one glitzy shop to be found in all of Mityana.

After the very long flight, my Benadryl-befuddled brain couldn't tell me if it were day or night. The airline ticket used the twenty-four-hour time method, but my iPhone clock used the twelve-hour.

When I read the time as 9:28, and with all the lights and glitz in the terminal, I was sure it was morning. Only later did I discover it was actually night! My body clock was completely out of kilter! Thankfully, I figured that out before my next flight.

The Entebbe airport was night and day different from Qatar. Upon entering the rather shabby terminal, I began the long process of what seemed an endless series of checkpoints. Each one required showing my passport, visa, vaccination cards, and COVID-19 testing, all while wearing the allegedly essential face mask.

My escaping breath fogged the inside of my glasses, impeding a clear navigation through the crowd as I trudged along to find the next checkpoint. The warm and moist air only aggravated my sense of suffocation. My lenses were about as foggy as my brain!

Then came the gutsy task of grabbing my two fifty-pound stuffed-to-the-hilt suitcases off a moving belt to haul to the taxi that would be waiting for me outside. My first attempt left me reeling!

It was a wrestling match for sure, but a tall Ugandan gentleman saw my plight and was kind enough to grab them for me on the next round and with little effort on his part. He helped me secure them on the luggage cart, and after heartily thanking him, I plodded along to find an exit to the exterior.

Outside I was affronted by various Ugandan taxi drivers holding up papers with written names. As I sauntered the concrete ramp, I squinted and searched the placards displayed carefully, but my name was nowhere to be seen.

After patiently waiting and peering intensely at each new driver, I finally saw a small-statured obscure man walking toward the terminal. As I stared in the distance, I was delighted to faintly make out my name on the paper in front of him!

I enthusiastically waved my arm, and as he came closer, he looked a little dismayed at seeing the two large suitcases I was lugging on the cart. He was clearly much more daunted, however, at the actual task of lifting them off the cart! With about as much difficulty as I had, he hauled the heavy luggage as we walked some distance through the dusty parking lot before arriving at his auto.

I was a bit apprehensive seeing the small older vehicle as I entered its dilapidated seats. The steering wheel on the opposite side confused me. As we started on our way, I gripped the seat tightly.

"This crazy guy is driving on the wrong side of the road!" I thought loudly to myself. It took a while to calm my inner nerves as I suddenly remembered I needed to orient myself to the British norm of left-sided driving.

After about fifteen minutes of driving through rundown shops, I was pleasantly surprised to see a palm tree-lined road that led to my nice but modest Entebbe Palm Hotel. I received a very warm welcome.

The young hotel assistant awkwardly wrestled with my cumbersome baggage as he led the way to my room up three flights of stairs.

Once inside the spacious room, I began to squeamishly check the bedding, mattress, and bathroom! I was relieved that all seemed clean and good.

My nerves were beginning to calm down until I saw teensy black bugs on the coffee table. Shocked, I began to furiously kill as many bugs as I could! With vengeance I smashed and smattered my fingers on them, crushing their bodies to smithereens!

I then began to examine the corpses as closely as I could not being able to determine what kind of bug it was. I took photos of the dead ones, and enlarged the pics. Finally I breathed a sigh of relief, "Whew!" They were only minuscule sugar ants!

Reassured but exhausted and very grateful for the heavenly hot shower, I plopped onto the surprisingly comfortable bed. It was so quiet that I fell asleep before I could get myself dressed to go downstairs and indulge in the delicious-looking oriental meal I had seen on the restaurant menu.

At about 7:00 p.m., I was abruptly awakened by a loud laughing ruckus. "Oh great!" I mumbled to myself. I supposed by the loud voices that men were drinking below my room and that it would, no doubt, last late into the night.

I decided it best that I not leave and hunkered down inside. I rummaged my bags and found some squashed nuts and prunes that I had stuffed into one of the pockets, and I hungrily imbibed.

Surprisingly, the loud male voices ended abruptly at 8:00 p.m. With my hunger satisfied, I sank into a deep and very sound sleep.

Beautiful unique bird songs woke me up the next morning as the sun filtered through the curtains. I felt refreshed having slept so soundly. I freshened up to exit my room and check the restaurant below.

The waitress explained that loud ruckus the night before was only a father and son enjoying a very rambunctious game of pool below me. I chided myself silently for resorting to my crude meal of prunes and smashed nuts when I could have enjoyed a great Asian meal!

I began to get excited at the prospect of seeing Kakembo and Joseph for the first time! They were renting a friend's van to pick me up, and I promised to treat them to a good restaurant meal for lunch.

Kakembo's texted response using the American idiom to my invitation was, "Awesome!" No doubt, in his mind, good restaurant eating was a privilege for the rich that he was eager to experience for himself!

I waited in the open seating area at a table below, enjoying the palm trees, unique flowers, and birds. It was a relaxing scene and balmy weather to take in.

While gazing at some beautiful birds in a tree, I finally caught a glimpse of the two brothers entering from around the corner. I recognized them right away, and I couldn't help but eagerly jump up to run and give a tight bear hug to each of them! There were definitely no inhibitions on my part!

My arms encircled both of these dear slightly-built sons in Christ with no problem as we posed for photos. A lot of lighthearted jokes, laughing, and hugs followed with great joy at finally seeing each other in person!

I made good on my promise of a delicious restaurant meal for the guys. Kakembo and Joseph ordered an appetizing lunch of pork ribs and fries, and I finally got to relish a tasty Asian ginger chicken meal! Despite their very slim waistlines, they easily packed down those generous plates of food and mango slushies without a bit of a struggle. It did my heart good to see them eating heartily and enjoying the tempting and well-prepared food.

We had much to talk about! Our respective native accents didn't seem to hinder our gabbing, and our sincere affections richly seasoned our conversation.

The large city of Entebbe had some nice sections, and I wanted the guys to see the local zoo there since they had never seen one. It was unfortunately pretty run down, and as we followed a volunteer guide, I became actually sorry we had stopped.

Even though we saw interesting animals, the lions and several other animals looked like they were near starvation. I didn't let it be known, but I was eager to leave, as I have an extra sensitive heart when it comes to animals. The outlying areas revealed the prevalent poverty that plagues this country. It wasn't only the animals who were suffering.

The paved roadways were drivable in and out of Entebbe, and some areas of the city were very nice. About two hours out of the city, I noticed the roads became increasingly worse. I was amazed at how many nomadic cattle herdsmen we passed, leading their long-horned cattle to whatever grass and water they could find.

In passing villages the dirt roads were lined with shanty bungalow shops selling all kinds of wares. Piles of clothing from China, some with name brands, were displayed, along with vegetable and fruit stalls, meat shops with dust-covered raw beef or chicken hanging on hooks, along with electronics and mechanics.

Poor little goats on short chains along the sides of the roadways were struggling to find patches of grass, and chickens imprisoned in tiny cages were piled high atop each other.

We stopped at one village as sellers of cooked food approached our van windows. Joseph and Kakembo bought some fresh fire-cooked chicken on a stick while the next live squawking chicken was being carried by its feet over to the chopping block. At least it was fresh!

I tried a fire-roasted green banana or "matooke," which had a bit of tartness with a fire-roasted flavor. Bottled water was also sold.

As we neared the Mityana area, the roads shifted into crater-like back streets! The lack of rain caused clouds of red clay dust to rise from the road and settle everywhere. I was amazed that any vehicle, bike or boda boda (motorbike), could withstand the numerous cavernous potholes!

As vehicles passed us, we were required to keep our windows closed despite the dank heat. Even my Kuhl brand high-tech breathable fabric shirt didn't stop my damp perspiration. So much for technology!

I had previously decided a hotel room was best suited for me during my stay. Floor space was valuable at the orphanage, and I didn't want to rob a much-needed mattress.

Kakembo had previously inspected the room I had reserved to ensure its cleanliness. When we turned onto the narrow stretch of roadway leading to the hotel, I was appalled at its condition! The very narrow road was lined with shanty lean-tos and half-naked children. It had sharp deep edges, making it very hard to navigate without running into a child or goat along the way.

After a short way, we entered into what was a hand-excavated driveway and gate entrance to the Makan Hill Resort Hotel. It felt like a haven, with surrounding trees shielding us from the poverty outside the gate and shading the entry to the hotel.

Once again, I received a warm hotel staff greeting, as Kakembo and Joseph unloaded my weighty cargo. My room was quite a bit smaller than the previous one, but most importantly, it was clean! I settled into my confined space and gave the overpacked suitcases to the guys to take back to the orphanage.

I spent some time explaining the contents. They were filled with crafts, clothes, medicines, difficult-to-find items like plastic ponchos, Kool-Aid, nuts, chicken bouillon, onion, garlic, and all kinds of seasonings and spices, peach and other teas, chicken fajita soup mixes, foil packed tuna and chicken, hot chocolate mixes, and many other items we Americans deem as just run-of-the mill essentials.

I included night lights, multi-tool pocket knives, and even included jewelry wear for the girls and a special gold set for Brenda. There were sanitary pads, toiletry items, and jump ropes, yo-yos, blow-up beach balls, and toys for the children.

After buying a CD player, the kids and adults really enjoyed the various Christian music CDs that were included. Children's songs gave the kids a reason to dance as music is an important part of their lives.

I laughed when Kakembo weeks later provided me photos of the kids dressed in the T-shirts I brought. They had used fabric paint for the words "Blessed Hope," the name chosen for our orphanage. The kids all rocked with the colorful dollar store sunglasses! Even Kakembo rocked! Bob and I later had fun sending a video of us rockin' in our sunglasses as well.

The guys were overwhelmed at all the new and tantalizing oddities I had stuffed in that luggage, but they knew that the dispensing of these gifts would have to be in an organized and time-sensitive way so as not to cause too much kiddo commotion! I was amazed at how coordinated they were with the children. We hugged goodbye and planned our next morning visit at the orphanage.

I was pleased with the fan included in my room since the AC was non-existent. The bathroom left much to be desired! One starchy white towel, a teeny bar of soap, one half roll of thin toilet paper, a mirror, sink, and a shower without enclosure or curtain were all walled within a small, tiled cubicle sans an exhaust fan. Each shower left water and mist saturating the toilet seat, mirror, and floor.

Trying to remember to turn on the small water heater fifteen minutes prior to showering was a challenge. I had my washed undies hanging over the sink edges and toiletries strewn on the floor in the uncomfortably confined space. The bed, however, was comfortable, and the mosquito netting was a bonus. Yet it was the fan that was a real plus!

I slept like a baby through the night, and the next morning I savored the motel-provided breakfast with its unique seasonings. They offered scrambled eggs, Irish potatoes, sautéed spinach, sausage links, and mango or orange juice. I ate well while listening to the English Ugandan TV news and managed to wrap a couple of sausages in a napkin for the guys to sample later.

At 9:30 a.m., I expectantly opened the door. Both young men with their beautiful radiant smiles greeted me, and my spontaneous response was to warmly bear-hug each of them. I was eager to see the new orphanage home and especially the kids!

I couldn't help but compare the horrifically pot-holed hotel access road with the orphanage's smooth entry road. Joseph, Kakembo, Brenda, and Nagawa's blood, sweat, and tears carved this into being themselves, after clearing trees and bushes! No doubt lots of tough elbow grease in hot, humid conditions was necessary for that endeavor, not to mention their daily bruises and sore muscles!

I was surprised at seeing how many homes were already being built in close proximity. Owners had utilized this orphanage road to access their own building projects. The nearby red brick oven that was used to provide bricks for the house looked like a giant anthill.

The brick wall that encompassed the nicely finished orphanage home was also encased with cement and even showcased some decorative paint touches. The house was finished with a lovely spring green pastel color. Iron bar doors provided good security from the very common thievery and break-ins.

Kakembo reminded me the children had friends as I looked in amazement at the the very long array of kids in the photo. The house looked marvelous! I was so proud of Kakembo's incredible achievement and very hard work!

Exuberant Welcome

As Kakembo unlocked the large metal-crafted entry gate, I heard the commotion behind it. Upon entering, I was swept up in a tsunami of beautiful brown children with bright eyes and white smiles holding out their loving arms and chanting in unison "Welcome, Mom! Welcome, Mom!" Delightfully overwhelmed, I caught sight through my teary eyes of the background balloons and posters displayed, saying, "We love you, Mom!"

There are no adequate words to describe the love and joy I felt in those moments! I had only wished that Bob could have been there and that I would have had longer arms to embrace all these beautiful children! After the heartfelt welcome, the kids and I were brought inside.

They led me to a foldable lawn chair in the sitting room just for me to sit in and prop my legs up. It was the only piece of furniture in the whole house.

Little Ryan would come and crawl up on my lap while I took some selfies with his winsome smiles. His adorable laugh had me grinning from ear to ear.

At last the gifts came out for the children to see as some held up the clear plastic bags for the others to get a look at what was inside. Of course, I had to grab Joseph and Kakembo for a photo shoot!

The gifts would be handed out in an orderly fashion so that one activity could be performed at a time. The first gifts to come out were the large coloring books and crayons. The older children would come up one by one to show me their finished masterpieces with gleaming looks of pride on their faces.

Older kids who could read English took turns coming to the front to read a page from one of the storybooks I brought. The children would sit quietly on mats while straining to see the pictures.

I made a video with all the kids waving at Bob as they yelled "We love you Dad Bob!" He enjoyed the video immensely.

Then it was Bible lesson time. Joseph would teach in English while Kakembo translated into the Luganda language. The two young men were animated and persuasive as the kids listened attentively.

The lesson was about two Old Testament characters, one being Saul, who received God's material blessings. However, Saul forgot the Lord, and became disobedient, thereby losing all that the Lord had given him.

Then there was David, who thanked the Lord for His blessings and kept his dedication and love for Him throughout his life. God blessed him greatly with much more!

The moral of the story: Do not take God's blessings for granted! Follow Him with your whole heart, be thankful, and enjoy His blessings. Kakembo and Joseph were living examples of that!

The midday meal was prepared outdoors over a wood fire, with Kakembo, Joseph and Nagawa doing the outdoor cooking. Thankfully it was a day without rain!

There would be posho, a stiff maize flour porridge, with beans, tomatoes, and some rice. It was quite the ordeal to get the food served up from the floor in the kitchen area for all the kids.

I was grateful to see that Nagawa had a good friend, Beatrice, who was staying to help with all the children. More than just one woman was required to attend to all those children's needs!

Beatrice had such a gentle touch with the kids, and provided valuable assistance. She also provided Nagawa with someone to talk to from a woman's perspective!

At last, the adults were able to serve themselves, as they ate sitting on the floor as well. I, the only one sitting on a chair, found it to be very tasty and a meal that would stick to my ribs all afternoon!

That evening, the boys had arranged to show me the nearby Lake Wamala. This name was derived from the last king of a historical dynasty, King Wamala, who is said to have disappeared into the lake. Legend says his spirit resides in the lake area, and spiritual rituals are conducted on the islands in the inlet. Fishermen use small boats to fish for catfish, tilapia, and lungfish on the lake. However, surrounding villages conveniently dump their waste into those waters.

We stopped at the shore with a neighboring shanty village behind us. Kakembo mentioned the village was known for practicing witchcraft, and he and Joseph were hoping to have an evangelistic crusade there in the near future.

As we stepped out to talk to local fishermen, children gawked at me. I was a strange sight to them with my white skin and light hair, a rarity in that location.

A man nearby was crawling across the street on his hands and knees. It gave me an eerie feeling as I gazed at him.

It was getting dusk, but despite that, Joseph asked one of the fishermen if he could pay for a short boat ride for us. The man provided life jackets that even had fluorescent patches for nighttime, so apparently, boat excursions were a side business.

As we precariously boarded into the old wooden boat, we began our venture with only a dim light at the bow of the boat. Kakembo confessed the murky black water of the lake terrified him as he confided he couldn't swim. The darkness was setting in, so it only added to the feeling of vulnerability as the boat slid slowly into the blackness ahead.

We joked back and forth as I assured him I could swim, and if the boat sank, I promised that I would rescue him! It was a fun short adventure, but Kakembo did seem very relieved when we finally came back to shore. No doubt, the local legend of the king's spirit living in the lake gave a certain sense of foreboding. As we drove away, I looked back at the shanty town and was left with a sober feeling. How did these poor and spiritually lost villagers survive with such meager hopes?

The next day, I arrived at the orphanage just about bath time for the kids. An outdoor shower was a nice addition to rinse off the dirt before entering the house.

As we walked around back, I was taken aback by all the little brown bodies running around in the buff! I was glad for the privacy wall around them, but I had to put my head back and let out an unrestrained belly laugh. Before I knew it, I had about ten little nudies running to surround me with their precious hugs! Oh, what joy those kids bring!

The days went quickly, but I so enjoyed watching these handsome sons in Christ around the children. There were fun times watching Joseph show off his jump rope skills with one leg while Kakembo demonstrated his deft movements with the soccer ball. The children loved them, and they kept the children busy through these organized game times.

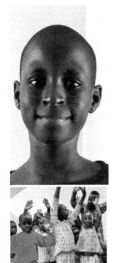

As Joseph was organizing a game much like hopscotch, Kakembo and I watched and visited as we reminisced about all that had happened in just one very short year. Then it was Bible stories, meal preparation and feeding, clean up, bath times, and bedtime.

Nagawa was constantly busy trying her best to keep the floors clean as she ensured that every child dipped their feet in a small tub of water, dried off, and then sat down on the mats provided in the sitting room.

All three adults had a firm handle on controlling the children in a very organized way, and the children really did love them. I had wished Brenda could have been there, knowing her love for the kids and hard work were dearly missed.

One afternoon while resting in the sitting room, I chuckled as I watched streaking little brown bodies running gleefully past the door window. They were thoroughly amused as they chased each other before bath time, no doubt raising plenty of dust while doing so.

Nagawa finally had time to shed her work clothes, and she came into the sitting room looking so lovely in her African blue dress. I was grateful to see that Kakembo ensured she had something pretty to wear! She sat on the floor by my side while she peeled and gave me slices of sweet mangos.

We had a dear chat together as well as some tears as she talked about her previous life with her cruel uncle. She spoke of how thankful she was to have found a refuge at Blessed Hope. They were special moments, and I appreciated the time she took to be with me. It was another beautiful memory to cherish. I couldn't help but feel I belonged there!

Time went quickly. Kakembo and Joseph took time and effort for me to see the beautiful countryside of Uganda that even they hadn't seen. It added to the memories and made me realize that Uganda does indeed have beautiful, picturesque views.

I was amazed at some of the orangutans we saw on the sides of a mountain roadway. There were even beautiful mountain views of crater lakes and a waterfall! Yes, even Uganda fed my "mountain mama" spirit. Kakembo knew I'd love it!

Feb.15,2023

I was sad even thinking about the time come to say our goodbyes. I truly felt as if I was leaving a big chunk of my heart and wished we weren't separated by such a vast amount of land and oceans! The boys were silent on the drive back to Entebbe. I had one more night at the airport hotel before my very long and grueling return flight home.

We gave our last hugs. Kakembo held on much longer and tighter than usual, and when I saw his tearful eyes, I couldn't hold back my tears. Why are goodbyes so hard!? I was so thankful we could continue to chat via Facebook Messenger, but it wouldn't be quite the same. Those last hugs were very meaningful. I knew our heart connections and the story the Lord was writing would continue.

I love every live video Kakembo sends, allowing me to relive my moments there. The recent video showing laughing and excited kids chasing a neighbor's escaped chicken inside their walled courtyard brought me heartwarming memories of their beautiful, gleeful faces.

I am reminded of this orphanage's many needs when I see pictures of the children gleaning firewood, fetching water, and walking the dangerous road to school.

The needs of food, medical treatments, clothing, school fees, or supplies will never end. In every step of the way, they have dedicated, God-fearing caregivers leading the way. Kakembo and his team are doing everything they can to raise these children to become God-fearing, responsible adults who will contribute to their communities.

Having a sensitive heart for the poor, Kakembo doesn't stop reaching out in any way he can to help those who suffer. There are many poor but very few who help.

Please pray the Lord continues to create new resources for the needs of these children to become all that He wants them to be. Also, pray for God's special blessing on him as he begins Bible courses to increase his expertise and knowledge of the Word of God and become equipped as a pastor and evangelist.

I'm blessed to see how God continues to bring His connections through Blessed Hope. It has only been recently to see His divine connections to a dear sister in Christ, Karen Odom Howington, who sees Joseph as her son in Christ! She has a similar story as I do with how the Lord led her to a heart connection with Joseph.

How deep His love! Only God! What beautiful stories we have to share together, knowing that we understand each other in ways no one else could.

It could be that the Lord is leading you as well into this divine connection. Please know that all proceeds of this book will go back into the support of this beloved God-given orphanage.

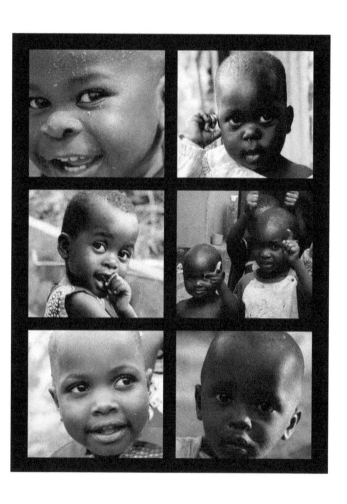

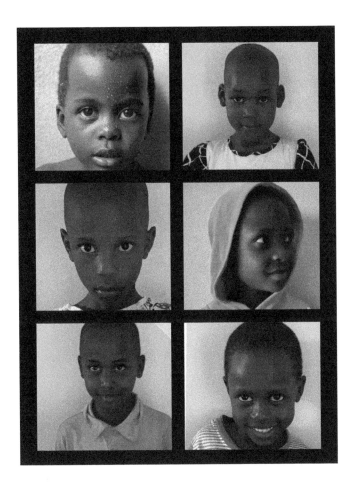

Be blessed! Be assured of His goodness and blessings. He is and will continue to do His good will. He starts and finishes.

> "God, who began the good work within you, will continue His work until it is finally finished on the day when Christ Jesus returns" (Phil. 1:6 NLT).

"If you help the poor, you are lending to the Lord—
He will repay you! (Prov. 19:17 NLT)

My husband and I have learned so much about giving and receiving. However, I would fail my calling in life if I didn't share the greatest gift of all, the salvation of our souls and spirits given freely to us through the sacrifice of the cross of Jesus Christ. Through His sacrifice, he has freed us to quit relying on our own goodness and instead receive His purity through the gift of salvation by enabling us to be free from the condemnation of sin.

When we ask for His forgiveness for our life's impurities and offenses toward Him and others, He forgives and cleanses us and replaces our unrighteousness with His righteousness. It's a divine gift!

Receive it freely and begin to experience His divine connection to your heart. You won't be disappointed! I promise, and so does He!

John 3:16 says, "For God so loved the world that He gave His one and only son that whoever believes in Him shall not perish but have eternal life." Wow! The gift of eternity! Don't pass it up!

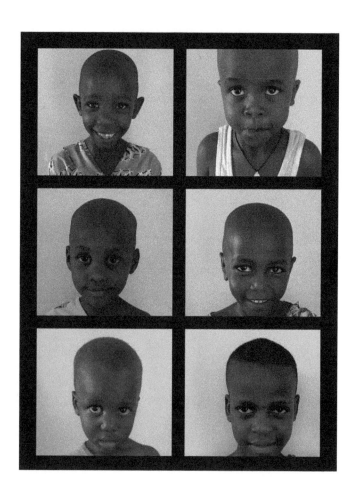

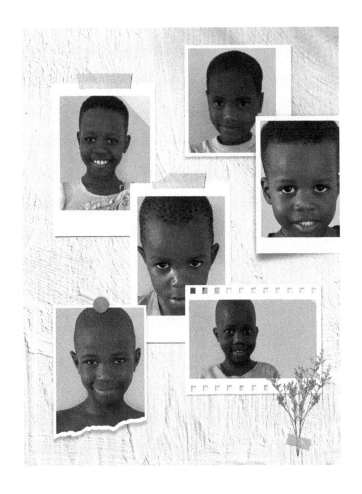

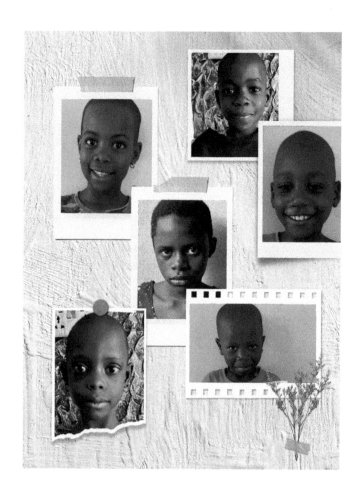

Sharing a dream.
Happy together

Afterword:

An Ebola outbreak has begun in Uganda as of October 2022. In addition to typhoid and malaria, the Ebola virus, which causes severe bleeding and organ failure, is now also a potential threat. Please pray for the safety and protection of the children and adults at Blessed Hope.

Kakembo is very grateful for the hard work and love that Nagawa gives freely to the children. She has become such a valuable team member as a sister in Christ, and works very hard for their well-being.

However, this "mountain mama" felt a little nudge was perhaps needed toward planting the idea towards marriage into my son-in-Christ's mind. I realized soon, however, that I didn't need to plant that idea! It was already there!

Nagawa had came down with a serious case of typhoid and was hospitalized for some days. Kakembo stayed by her side and soon realized how much he loved her. He then revealed to me he wanted to marry her! I was delighted!

After her recovery, he created a very special occasion for her when he proposed...a date night at a nice restaurant. A legal marriage will come first in February, but a Ugandan wedding reception will be the wonderful next event to unfold!

Bob and I won't be able to participate in person, but I am promised many photos and videos of this beautiful couple and the joyful occasion. It makes this "mountain mama" blissfully blessed!

For more information about ways to help Blessed Hope
Orphanage, please email

verna_r_deno@yahoo.com

Verna is also available for speaking engagements.

CPSIA information can be obtained
at www.ICGtesting.com
Printed in the USA
LVHW010044170623
749928LV00006B/10